"This book is a real find. Not a how-to manual, or a step-by-step action plan, it instead offers an unyielding glimpse into the hearts, minds and behaviors of seniors. The vignettes are raw and touching. Touch love for seniors, those that care for them, and those that advise them. The book is easy to read, and hard to put down. Order it now!"

— Marilee Driscoll, Plymouth, MA
www.MarileeDriscoll.com

"Your book really brings out the emotional side of the (senior) issue and makes it very personal. You did an incredible job of capturing the emotions."

— Nancy Maline, Editor
Agent Sales Journal, FL

"I loved Unwrapping the Sandwich Generation. It helped me to better understand my parents. I bought copies for all my children to help them understand me!"

— Richard P. Cook,
Virginia Beach, VA

"Sue Cunningham has written a little gem of a book that is both insightful and practical. Drawing on her years of experience working with the children of aging parents, she has collected a series of pithy stories and observations that simultaneously inspire and educate. Unwrapping the Sandwich Generation is a recommended read for professionals and children of elders alike!"

— John Paul Marosy, President
Bringing Elder Care Home LLC, MA
www.bringingeldercarehome.com

T0163991

"I just finished reading your wonderful book Unwrapping the Sandwich Generation and found it fascinating and absorbing. Since we're going through some harrowing experiences with our 97-year-old uncle, the book was helpful in more ways than one."
— C.T., VA

"Your book, Unwrapping the Sandwich Generation, is delightful, informative, realistic and easy to read. It raises awareness of a common (aging) problem in today's society. Thank you for opening eyes and hearts."
— H.W., VA

"Unwrapping the Sandwich Generation should be a bit of required reading for counselors of seniors who want to be knowledgeable of and familiar with all the things that are happening to the aging population. A must read for children of aging parents who are becoming more dependent than they want to become. A "coffee table" tome for continuing care centers where we now allow our parents to reside, this book will be in use for some time to come for it is us."
— Fred L. Adair, Ph.D., LPC, NCC
Professor Emeritus, The College of William and Mary

UNWRAPPING THE
SANDWICH GENERATION

Life Vignettes About Seniors

And Their Adult Boomer Children

Susan Cunningham

You are not alone

UNWRAPPING THE SANDWICH GENERATION

Susan Cunningham

Life Vignettes About Seniors
And Their Adult Boomer Children

Cover design and book layout by Bonnie Bushman
bbushman@bresnan.net

Morgan James Publishing, LLC
1225 Franklin Ave. Ste 325
Garden City, NY 11530-1693
800-485-4943
www.MorganJamesPublishing.com

Habitat
for Humanity®
Peninsula
Building Partner

Cunningham, Sue.
    Unwrapping The Sandwich Generation/ Sue
Cunningham
    ISBN 0-9768491-9-4

Dedication

To Roy and Rob...

you are the wind beneath my wings.

Table of Contents

Introduction

Thank you for having an interest in the generation that set the stage for the rest of us. It is my sincere desire that you sit back, read these vignettes and come away with a feeling. What kind of feeling is up to you.

These are stories about and for seniors and their adult children. They are written to help us all appreciate what it is to "age" or "grow old" or "become a senior" or whatever you call becoming more and more dependant on others. None of us, absolutely none of us, want to grow old and dependent. But as the saying goes, it is better than the alternative – most of the time.

These life-inspired stories are to help you understand what seniors experience as they age.

They are written with many family members in mind. Some stories are from the adult child's point of view, others from the senior's point of view. You will read about happiness, sadness, acceptance, rejection and many, many other feelings and emotions as we all travel the senior journey.

I received my inspiration from actual events and real people but places, names and circumstances have been changed for obvious reasons.

Please make this *your* book. As you read, jot down your thoughts. Then go back after a while and see if you still have the same thoughts and feelings. This is also a good book to share with friends or family members going through some of their own senior issues.

It's meant to be a book that can be opened anywhere and enjoyed wherever you start. Delight in one chapter at a time or read it straight through. Savor it slowly story by story much as you would enjoy a comfortable sweater and hot drink by a warm fire. Expect some stories to inspire you. Others will make you chuckle or laugh out loud. I even hope to invoke a few tears. I'm certain you will see examples of friends, or family members, or maybe your own reflection will bounce off a page or two.

I hope you enjoy reading the vignettes as much as I enjoyed putting them together for you. But my hope is that you see yourself or someone you love within the scope of the story. Maybe it will give you pause, insight, and another way to view and respond to the seniors in your life during this uncharted and unknown area of their life. No one really *expects* to grow old. So when we find ourselves there it is somewhat of a surprise even if we have been surrounded by older people all our lives. It is still somewhat of a strange phenomena when it happens to *you*. As my dear friend Ginny said, "One day I woke up and I was eighty. How did that happen without my noticing?" Indeed.

Susan Lea Cunningham; April 2005

Speaking Loudly Without Saying A Word

She had a raspy voice, almost as if she had something in her throat but it was perfectly all right for it to be there. A little "off-putting" to the listener, but of no consequence to the speaker.

Noticing the obvious signs of Parkinson's disease, the shaking, her nervous look, her head seeming to rest precariously on her stooped shoulders, I asked, "Can you walk ok?" Slowly her head turned, just enough to get the questioner in her peripheral view and with eyes twinkling, the "thing" in her throat allowed her

to say, " Well, I'm not as frisky as I used to be."
The seam of a mouth turned up at each corner
as if to cradle those words before they escaped.
However, the corners quickly straightened out
and she was quiet again. She retreated back into
her world, obviously a place where she enjoyed
being, a place seemingly much more comfortable
than the retirement community conference room
where she currently sat.

Her audience, consisting of a marketing
counselor for the retirement community and a
worried, frustrated, only child vacillating between
anger and frustration, couldn't help but laugh out
loud. Her comments were so contradictory for a
person who couldn't communicate verbally very
well, whose hairpiece was askew, whose clothes

were quality but ill fitting and who didn't seem to really care where she was or who was with her.

Or did she?

Maybe she was actually the one in control with her audience observing someone who knew exactly what she wanted and did not want. The three of them, mother, daughter and counselor were sitting in the conference room of the retirement community. You know, the place to "retire," where you can "finally do what you always wanted to do." But it was definitely not what she wanted, and she was making it crystal clear to her daughter without speaking a single word.

Do we ask our parents to do what is best for them…or best for ourselves?

Who Is Making This Decision, Anyway?

A friend is always the best crutch when you don't really need one. She came with a friend. A comfortable crutch of a friend. She didn't take up much room in the chair. A pixie haircut fell into place on her head. She announced herself to be "a widow of one year, five months TODAY." She is still grieving, worried, and angry with her four sons. When she entered the room, she wore a blue windbreaker zipped as far up as it could go. It was obviously keeping out more than just the cold February wind and rain. You could tell her smile, once very warm and real, was now about to shatter like a fragile piece of porcelain.

It stayed on her face through sheer will power and she looked tired and strained because of it. Explaining why her sons wanted her "to find a home, which is so silly because I'm only sixty-eight," she said she would not move out of town to be closer to them because "If they can't take five minutes to call me once or twice a week, how in the world would they treat me if I lived in town nearer to them? Besides," she sniffed, "I don't want to be dependent on them for anything, much less a phone call."

The anger was taking form.

She's diabetic and has been for over fifty years. Self medicating. No problem. That is, as long as "a spell" doesn't come up without warning. Afraid of not being found until the next day or whenever someone happens to check up on her ("God knows my sons won't!"), she seeks freedom. Freedom from worry and freedom from dependence on neighbors. Strangely enough, I sense she is quite at home with her fifty-year companion that this disease has become. They have learned to live together in understanding if not harmony, with one still overpowering the other. And the other acquiesces, as she must. She has no control.

She cannot control her husband's death. She cannot control her sons' apparent lack of interest. She cannot control the disease. She cannot control their constant nagging that she find "a retirement home."

However, she can control where she lives. Control has to take form somehow and getting the children off her back is as easy as talking to someone in the retirement community who will see she is too young, too healthy, too independent to live there. Surely, they will agree with her.

But she is also scared, insulin dependent, and tired of taking care of the house. Now what?

Call your parents today. Even if you don't get along. Call them. Even for five minutes. Check on them. One day someone is going to have to check on you.

Invisibility On The Phone

On the phone he sounded nice. Tired, but nice. His vocabulary skipped along hand in hand with intelligent words, big words, long words but still easy on the listener's ear. He was happy that I called. Later in the conversation I found out why.

I never had the opportunity to speak with his wife on the phone. We all met late that afternoon. Yes, he agreed, they would like to come see the apartment. An apartment in the floor plan they wanted had finally become available. One problem: It is in Assisted Living. They wanted Independent Living.

When I met them later that day, I could see as well as hear his fatigue. A little bent over, he walked with a cane and a limp. All these months that we had been talking on the phone all he ever talked about were *her* needs, never his own. I never had a clue *he* had a single one.

His left leg shuffled itself along as if it were a reluctant passenger rather than an integral part of the walking process. His eyes were slightly closed, very red and set deep in their sockets. The tearing that I attributed to the cold weather was in fact, part of his weariness. Why was this obviously intelligent, charming man so tired? Oh! It's because he's in love!

They have been married for sixty years. She has had Parkinson's disease for fifteen years. Fifteen years! That means she succumbed to its clutches when she was in her late sixties. Much too young! Incontinent, unable to control her hand to drink an offered cup of coffee, she needs constant attention. Daily linen care. Daily meals. Daily checking. At home she still is trying to cook all their meals with her grandmother's cast iron skillet and manipulate it around her constant companion, her walker.

Her body may need constant attention but not her brain. Surprisingly, this World War II Wac can still offer a grip to rival many men her age. She has a quick wit and a take on her surroundings with the accuracy of a periscope doing a 360.

But it becomes painfully obvious why her devoted puppy of a husband is so bone weary. He confesses, "I have to go behind her on everything. And I'm so tired of having to do all the laundry.

But the main thing is that I'm scared: scared she is going to burn down the house when she goes into the kitchen."

Tearing, red-ringed eyes look up to me. He puts his caneless hand over mine and asks, "Can you please help us?"

Sometimes the time to make a decision about moving to an alternative living community is so obvious, you can't see it for all the daily living.

Hidden Agendas

He is the son-in-law. Short, both in stature and sentence structure. He is late to the meeting, rubbing his hands with their chewed fingernails against his brown, too-tight khaki pants. His tie chokes his red, puffy neck. He has sweated through his collar and it's seeping into his tie. He looks down as he shakes hands with the counselor. Although he has never visited the retirement community before, he looks familiar to the retirement counselor, he admits the counselor looks familiar as well but won't meet anyone's eye. What is going on here?

His wife has been to the retirement community before. So has his father-in-law and he didn't like it. But it is time. Time for "Dad to make the move." Dad doesn't want it. The daughter does. So does her husband. Everyone sits silently. Eyes are downcast. Each person clasps their own hands, fingers opening and closing. Silent movements. The silence is deafening. A decision about a person's life is about to be made. Three people but only one decision. Who wins?

Is everyone aware of the agenda?

Family Fires

The son, Sam, comes first, bringing a female friend. But he doesn't really need any help with this decision. She is there for what? Assurance, I think. Assurance that he is making the right move after all. "I'm hoping two heads are better than one," he offers with a smile. Shortly the other son, the quiet one, joins him.

He begins to describe his mother, his father and brother. After meeting with his family I appreciate that he is more on target than any adult child I have met under these trying circumstances. He slowly moves his head from side to side as he begins to try to paint a picture of his mom. No words escape a mouth that is making futile attempts to speak. Still the slow, deliberate movement of his head from side to side. At first he tries a few words... "She is stubborn. No, not stubborn; more controlling. No, more like mean as a snake." The last sentence proves to be the most accurate.

Dad, described as frail, caters to Mom. When I meet them I realize he is not just catering to her. He is keeping the peace. He is putting as much water on the family fire as he can while trying to not have another stroke.

Mom must weigh close to 225 lbs. Dad weighs in somewhere around 150. There is no question who wears the pants. She may be in a motorized "scooter," but she definitely makes everyone else march to the beat of her drum. Except Sam. He says he is too much like her. Someone needs to be, I guess.

They have a ten-pound dog called "Son." Dad says, "That dog loves me more than my own sons do." I can see the hurt in the eyes of his boys. Finally, they can take it no longer. One of them blurts out.

"And just how many times has that dog taken you to the hospital?

Or picked you up when you fell at home?

Or put out the fire you started in the kitchen?

Or took your prescriptions to the pharmacy?"

Family members fall silent. Eyes brim with tears. Anger has arrived.

Mom silently and deliberately crosses her arms across her massive chest, one beefy arm very slowly folding itself over the other one. This gesture speaks volumes. Then she turns her head and her steely gaze toward her husband while Dad reaches over to pat her arm. Stubborn and controlling, indeed. The family fire is about to spontaneously combust.

The parents are so dependent on neighbors, friends, children, and the rescue squad. But they call themselves independent. The only real friend they have, they say, is their dog. The dog has become a tremendous obstacle in their lives but it is the only warmth they choose to cling to.

The retirement community their son selected does not accept pets. They won't move without the pet. One by one family members cross their arms or glare or plead, depending on who wants what. A ten-pound dog will determine their lifestyle, their future health and ultimately, their death.

What are the real reasons you can't talk to your children?

Speaking In Riddles

She is polite. She is well dressed, very well dressed and petite. She possesses and uses an excellent vocabulary. She is eighty years old, about a size six. She just came off the golf course and thought she would look into the concept of retirement living. She has a friend who lives in this community. She wants to see what that style of apartment looks like.

"I love my condo, but it's two stories and I'm getting concerned about the stairs."

Politely, the marketing counselor asks what Mrs. Size Six is seeking in a retirement community. Her response is "You tell me." Confused, I turn to the daughter for clarity. Mother answers once again: "We're just looking".

It is so difficult to help someone when they want you to guess what they need.

Free At Last,
Thank God Almighty

She is so beautiful. Her hair is obviously not the color given at birth but very stylish. I would have guessed she was about sixty years old but when her son introduced himself as her son, I had to ask, twice, "Y*our* mother? Your *mother?*"

He had to be in his middle fifties and shared that *he* was retired. So I looked back at her to see what I'd missed. Long polished nails, slim fingers that displayed a huge diamond on her left hand, and beautiful teeth ("All my own," she offered). She had a slim, almost athletic build, exquisite valuable jewelry around her neck and wrist and stylish clothes. No way could this gal be in her mid eighties.

Her husband had died only four months ago. She could talk about it much too easily. What was wrong here? She was getting ready to go to Hawaii next month with a girlfriend and excitedly announced to the room at large, "I can't wait to see what kind of men I meet!" She talked about what a wonderful lover her husband had been, how he had showered her with hugs and kisses. I watched her adult son squirm in his chair as she continued with a conversation much too intimate for her audience.

Her husband recently died of cancer after years of Parkinson's and Alzheimer's. She was now free. She would never, ever say those words out loud. But she was free.

Being a caregiver is a taxing, very much underappreciated job.

What's Wrong With This Picture?

Have you ever seen a situation that simply didn't look quite right? You can't put your finger on what doesn't fit. It's as if you have your undershirt on backwards. It's not really noticeable right away, it just feels funny until you realize the problem.

Well, something was "wrong with this picture." A white haired giant was being pushed into the office in a wheel chair. It looked wrong. It felt wrong. So, what was it? Like the backwards undershirt finally corrected, I realized it seemed as if he should have been doing the pushing, not the riding.

With his white hair and huge hands, he was strong and masculine looking. His hands looked frightening and gentle at the same time. They were the kind of hands you want to have on your side in a fight, not against you. He had a pair of the largest feet I had ever seen. Especially for a man not walking! He wore tennis shoes-very new, very white, with new laces. The laces still had the plastic tips on them. Had they ever touched the ground? If not, why not? What was this giant doing in a retirement community, let alone in a wheelchair?

A much smaller and obviously concerned man was pushing the wheelchair. "I got ya, Jack, ole buddy."

Willy, his best friend, was the pusher; Jack was the reluctant passenger.

Jack acknowledged the help but seemed pre-occupied, but with what? Not a smile for the friend. Not a nod of acknowledgement. Just a very strong handshake from those massive hands.

This man was on a mission.

Once he began to talk, he started with rapid-fire questions. I had seen this before. And I felt my own fear creeping into the room. I experienced this previously and I knew what was coming.

He did not mince words. He posed questions that most people ask in the second half of the meeting, not right away. His first staccato question was regarding quick, immediate availability of an apartment. He had no regard whatsoever about dining options or daily activities or fun trips. And he dismissed any concern about finances with a wave of the hand. "That doesn't bother me right now," Jack said.

I knew the signs. He seemed robust to us who didn't know him before his cancer.

"You wouldn't guess how much he has shrunk in the last few months," whispered Willy, the pusher, behind his hand. His eyes glistened over.

They were in the Army together. "When it was the Army Air Corps" as if that were when men were really men. "We wore the same uniform, didn't we, ole Buddy?"

"Yeah, Willy. We sure did." That was the longest sentence Jack had spoken so far.

Cancer will do that to you. It shortens your words and makes you get right to the point.

His eighty-two-year-old spine had been taken prisoner by disks that had begun to dissolve. The pain was now the encroaching leader of this new battle. This military trained giant was no longer standing straight and tall in his uniform, but continued his fight from a wheel chair when not leaning on Willy, his faithful Army buddy.

They left together. The small, healthy one smiling, so very glad to help. And the giant resigned to his fate.

Sometimes we wonder why a senior seems grumpy or negative. Do we know the whole story?

Marching Men, Old Soldiers

The daughter says this is her parents' decision. Yet, her parents wouldn't think of coming in the door without the daughter. "We don't make a move without her input." So, who is really the decision-maker here?

Mom has an obvious wig perched on her head. She is in a wheelchair and quite obviously experiencing pain from osteo-arthritis and osteoporosis. But what a spirit she possesses! In the middle of a sentence she suddenly pops out of her wheelchair and pronounces that it is "time for a pill" (an obvious pain pill). The family jumps to attention.

Dad calls her "sweetheart" all the time. Even when she is giving him driving lessons on navigating the wheelchair, he is patient and kind. She chuckles and says she will take away his driving license if he doesn't do better. All smile. But I feel that he would gladly give this chore away. He is tired and it shows.

He is a recently retired military chief, receiving 100% disability from his years in the military: "My old ticker, you know." That is the only way this Chief Petty Officer can afford retirement living. What has been done to our military men and women? Why must they be sick and dying before they can afford a basic lifestyle they have more than earned?

What are we doing about our retired military seniors? Why do they feel abandoned?

Southern Charm

This Southern, genteel, senior lady greets me at the front door of her huge, expensive, run down home with a beautiful smile. With a firm handshake, she looks me right in the eye and says, " I know you." My surprise and wide-eyed expression surely must give me away. Her family said she has dementia. As with many seniors with that diagnosis, it is often difficult to notice at first glance. I'm invited in with the grace one experiences only with the Southern women of that generation. Food, tea (sweetened, of course) and a comfortable place to sit are quickly and graciously offered and accepted.

She is correct. We met earlier and her eighty-plus-year-old memory recalls what my fifty-plus memory cannot. At least, not until later when her tinkling laughter, her sparkling eyes and sharp (albeit, short lived) humor rise to the surface to coat the whole room with Southern gentility. Of course! Now I remember. She came to visit a friend at a retirement community where I had been employed.

Where have all those graces hidden themselves from the younger generation? Where has the slow conversation retreated? You know the one; it rises with deliberate concern with questions about your ancestry, on both sides, of course. How you like your tea sweetened, before or after you add ice. And the correct "tea" spoon, not the one you use for cereal, for heaven's sake.

We slowly, rhythmically with an up and down cadence, dance with our words, and begin to talk about the reason for my visit. Her recent car accident left her with a totally demolished car but only a few broken toes. She was lucky this time. This is the second car accident in just a few months and, in a way, the family is relieved. They don't want her driving and now have a reason to "encourage" her to stop. Surprisingly, she agrees. She also agrees to a companion, a house cleaner and a driver.

But she does not agree to getting older and to being dependent. "This will do for now," she pronounces. The sweet smile slowly and almost mischievously spreads across smooth, almost wrinkle- free skin. The sparkle is still there.

Looking over her glass of tea, she asks, "Now why is it you're here, my dear?"

Things are not always what they seem to be. "Forgetfulness" wears many cloaks.

Love And Desperation

The daughter called with tears in her voice, "I have no life. You have to help me!" Almost before she said her name, she was telling me how her parents, whom she loves dearly, are consuming her life, her days, her thoughts, her hours, her car, and every other aspect of her life.

She has tried to talk to them but to no avail. Can I help? We agreed to meet at the parents' home. I'm greeted by one of the kindest faces I have seen on an elderly gentleman. I realize how much I miss my deceased father.

Mr. Farmer introduces me to his wife who is sweet, inviting and curiously inquisitive without being invasive. Their shallow-breathing daughter, Jackie, is smiling and generous. For the first time I see pleading eyes in Jackie's look and the look of dementia on Mom's face.

We talk for more than an hour. They are kind to their daughter as she explains that I'm there to see if there are some alternatives they may want to consider. Alternatives? Mom's curiosity shuts down! After further conversation these sweet people try to set me straight in a very kind way; they know they are "too dependent" on Jackie, but "everything is ok." Mom is emphatic. Jackie is emphatic. Dad is caught in the middle. I suggest perhaps the daughter may want to visit her newborn grandchild in a distant city. Mom and Dad hope she does and that she enjoys herself. Jackie explains she can't leave them when she is responsible for the doctor and hairdresser appointments, their tax preparations, trips to the grocery store, car repair shop, ad infinitum. "What would you do if I were not here and something happened?" she pleads.

Sweetly, gently, they listen with obvious love for their only daughter. (A son lives a few hours away and visits once a month.) "Honey," Dad soothingly explains, "the next door neighbor will come right over if we need anything while you are gone." Jackie reminds them that the neighbor is seventy-five years old, about to move out of her own home and brings cookies over from time to time. That is the extent of their neighborly relationship.

Reluctantly, they agree to interview some companies for home companions. Just once a week, just for a few hours. Jackie sighs. "At least it's a baby step," she says as we walk to the car. Because Mom had silent tears slipping down her cheeks when I left, I called a few hours later to check on her.

"Are they ok?" I ask. Jackie answers with more tears. "They changed their mind," she cried.

They had allowed Mom to make the decision.

Sometimes taking the reins is the kindest thing you can do when it becomes impossible for a senior to do it themselves. Knowing when and how is the secret.

Alone. Doing The Best You Can.

Mrs. Sanders called. It took over six phone calls before she conceded that "I know I need your services. I'm so tired of being ripped off." It hurts to hear that. Driving to her home I recall her reluctance, her hesitancy. I drive into a lovely neighborhood that is older but well maintained. Her home is no exception and reflects the neighborhood in age and maintenance.

Her husband died almost a year ago. She couldn't get anyone to return her calls: a lawyer, a realtor, a funeral parlor director. "They all think I'm old and stupid; I'm only old." She could have also said "and sharp as a tack."

Seniors get so tired of someone taking advantage of them. Handymen, lawn persons, lawyers, doctors pat them on the head and say they will get back with them. I fume as I hear how she has been treated. Alone, but with two local children who don't do much for or with her, she works out what she needs with my help. I present her with an assortment of attorneys, real estate and tax specialists, and a kind, young and very spiritual handyman. They all were hand picked to be patient, understanding and eager to be of assistance. None of them will charge for a consulting phone call. She is grateful and smiling when I leave.

I call back a few days later after letting my contacts know she is special. They await her call. The first to arrive is the handyman. He is with her for over two hours; "no charge."

He reports back to me. "She says she is tired of being ripped off. She wouldn't let me help her."

I could scream.

Fear is one of the biggest obstacles anyone has to hurdle. Being alone and single makes it even more difficult.

I'll Make My Own Decisions, Thank You!

Knocking on the expensive Assisted Living community apartment door, I hear a small voice say, "Come in." The door is locked for some unknown reason. Another squeaky comment slides under the door to greet my ears, " Just a minute." Grunts, shuffles, scraping and several attempts later, the door opens to allow me to see a smile, a walker and a short, bent over woman asking me to come in with the graciousness only an accomplished woman raised in the lap of luxury can pull off with such aplomb.

With more grunts, shuffling and muffled scraping of the walker over new carpet,

Mrs. Brown escorts me into her sparse but clean and sunny apartment. It takes several minutes for her to reach her destination…her favorite chair. She lines herself up backwards with her recliner, braces the walker and lets go with the ease of a trapeze artist, knowing she will land exactly where she aims. A large, satisfied grin announces her arrival to the chair that groans its disapproval.

Her slacks are too big and hang from her hips. The back of her hair has found a great resting spot at the top half of her recliner; her hair stays flat even when she gets up. I once heard an older woman call this "chair hair." I smile while I ponder the comment and decide I have to know Mrs. Brown better before we share that particular "senior moment."

Within a few minutes Mrs. Brown's bank trustee joins us. Mrs. Brown wants to change living arrangements... again! This would not be such a big deal except she has lived in four different communities within the last four years. And she is eighty-three years old!

I have been asked to meet her and find her a place to live that will meet with requirements. It is not long into the conversation before I realize that Mrs. Brown is quite used to getting her way and it is my opinion that her trustee is sick and tired of finding a place for this lady to live.

I prod for the reasons that she has been unhappy with her previous arrangements. After all, she has lived in an independent community, two conventional apartment complexes and one assisted living community.

Her reasons are:

1. "They rented to blacks, and if you are from the South, you would understand."

2. "The food was terrible."

3. "My daughter pulled me out without so much as a howdy-dee-doo. After all, I'm used to a nine- room home and living in an apartment is a very big adjustment."

As I glance in the direction of the trustee, I immediately decide this sweet lady will have to deal with the facts if I'm to help her. I explain:

1. "They" can rent to anyone and it's Federal law.

2. Maybe we need to think about meals on wheels or a personal chef.

3. We need to know if your daughter has any input with this decision today.

The sweet, charming, Southern woman metamorphosed before my eyes. "My daughter will not 'interfere' with this decision this time and she is going to have a rude awakening when she reads my will, anyway!"

This is going to be a very interesting case!

Change is difficult for anyone. But for a senior it can bring feelings of loss of control.

Manipulation Disguised As Caring.

The daughter called from Alabama. I could hear the frustration, a level of anxiousness and another level of "the last straw." But I didn't know where the last straw was taking us. I only knew she sounded as if she didn't know what else to do. Mom's attorney had given her my name. "Can you please help me?" she asked in a desperate voice.

Scene one: Mom in Virginia; a son living a few minutes away who doesn't have much to do with Mom. Mom says he's depressed, sister says he's a bum. His wife helps her mother-in-law, as she is able. Another daughter in New York thinks the Alabama daughter is over reacting. Alabama daughter and Virginia son have not spoken in ten years. As always, it is over trivial, long forgotten arguments. Alabama daughter wants to know if I will see Mom and help her find ways to socialize, get out more, etc. I said I would try.

Alabama daughter calls Mom and sets it up. I call Mom to confirm. All is ok. The day before our meeting Mom calls saying she wants to "renege." I suggest we meet anyway. Mom sighs a hesitant ok.

Scene two: Mom is lovely and lively for her eighty-plus years. Home is neat, very old but well kept. The neighborhood is going down slowly but the properties are neat. Mom eats too many frozen meals but does well with her medical checkups. She does not drive and depends on neighbors. Husband died almost eight years ago and we both shed a few "wifely" tears as she tells her story.

Seniors all want someone to listen to their story; their husband, their marriage, their trials together. We laugh, we cry, we share pictures, we hug.

All in all, she is content. The son, I conclude may indeed be a bum. But what mother will ever admit that. He won't answer his phone. He leaves town and doesn't tell her. He insists on doing her checkbook (the one and only thing he does for her) but does it only when and if he feels like it. Quietly she confesses, "He gets too upset if I ask someone else to do it." Manipulation.

She takes a Valium for her "anxiety." She confesses she had to take one to meet me.

Adjustment.

Friends call. Groceries are maintained. Doctor appointments are made and kept. The house is cleaned. Laundry is done.

Accomplishment.

But, a daughter is still worried and with due cause. Something will happen one day soon. Statistically, that is a fact. But, Mom is content. She takes her Valium. Son does the checkbook and friends come to call and check up on her. All is well while the giant sleeps.

I saw in the paper today where one of my first customers died. She was in her late eighties and left a very small apartment to two nephews in Europe. I wonder how many people will be at her funeral?

When adult children don't speak to each other, they become small children in large bodies. And they continue to be burdens to their aging parents.

Denial Is Not A River In Egypt.

Mrs. Schultz sounded like she couldn't be a day over sixty-five, strong, succinct, articulate. "I have a few issues," she tells me over the phone. What an understatement. She lives in a beautiful brick ranch house in one of the nicer parts of town. The yard and home are as meticulous as she is. Every room except, that is, the room where her husband "lives."

He is taking medication for the early stages of Alzheimer's. However, the family tells me that the doctor has never said *that* word; they "talk around it." They say maybe he is just forgetful.

Denial is a wonderful tool; but it only keeps the inevitable at bay when answers are needed.

Dementia Or Forgetfulness?

At eighty-two, my favorite uncle still stands tall at 6'3" although he used to be even taller. From a distance a slight hump in his back is the only indicator of his age. And all my life I've known him to have that shock of stark white hair, poker straight with not the slightest bit of wave or curl - just like his father.

Uncle Bobby is always the uncle with the easy smile and the generous hugs. He touches everyone. Sometimes his touch is in the extension of his hand to a stranger struggling with a suitcase or a bag of groceries. Sometimes his touch is a nod or a smile. The touch I like best is the soft kiss he places on my forehead. Often the kiss can be for a job well done or the companion to his teddy bear hugs. But the best kind is the kiss for absolutely nothing; for being alive, for being in the moment, for being me and for being him. He gives his gifts of love abundantly and freely.

He wasn't always this way. In his youth, prior to World War II, he was captain of the university football team. I've seen pictures of him, always tall and lean, running, running, running for all he's worth: The strap from his leather cap flying, left arm straight out ahead of him ready for the inevitable tackle, and the football held so tight against his right side it looks like an extension of his body. What a sight! What a guy! Tough, young, ready for the world.

Today he is a storyteller. He loves talking about his youth and how the hardships of the country during his childhood shaped him into the person that he is. Every time I see him, he tells the stories. Sometimes he tells the same story and sometimes he tells more of the same story. But best of all is when this giant of a man tells new stories; stories of hitchhiking, of riding the streetcar to take his dad lunch while on the job, of working for forty-cents an hour, of digging footings for the Texas power company in what he calls "the hot Texas prairie sun." I can almost see the waves of heat rising off the dusty, dry dirt and watch his shirt turn dark with sweat as he tells the story to us again.

This time it's different.

My favorite aunt, his wife, says he is beginning to repeat things. Funny. How can they tell? He has repeated these stories all my life. What makes this different?

He comes to visit us and I see for myself.

The stories are the same. The hot Texas prairie sun still blazes the same. But she's right; it is different.

This time when he tells the stories, the same wonderful, WWII stories, he forgets that he told us the same thing just two minutes before. As a result, he repeats the same thing over and over and over and over.

His short-term memory is gone. He can't remember where he put his shaving cream that he has kept in the same place for over fifty years. He can't remember where he is going after he gets all dressed up. He can't remember what day it is.

But he remembers the stories. And because I'm in his long-term memory, he remembers me. And he remembers to give soft kisses on the forehead and generous hugs. And I will always and forever remember him.

Our relatives and senior friends are a wealth of knowledge. Are you listening?

Under The Surface,
Loneliness.

She is not what I expected when she opened the door. I expected a strong voice and I was not surprised. I expected a firm handshake and was not surprised. I expected a smallish house and was not surprised.

But I did not expect what I saw. Petite, firm build, stylish gray hair and a clotheshorse with jewelry I instantly coveted. Martha was beautiful, smart, well dressed, articulate, funny, and also lonely, alone, not eating well and diabetic.

We started out as client and advisor. She was eighty but looked much younger. After two meetings, we were quickly growing to be friends and buddies. I had a very difficult time charging her for my services because I grew to love the time we spent together even when it was "chalked up to business" as she would say.

As my business grew, our friendship and love for each other grew. One day she told me that if she had been blessed with a daughter, she would want her to be just like me. I cried.

She gave her feelings so freely. I had never had anyone say that to me and I didn't know what to do with this wonderful woman and the precious gift she bestowed upon me. I didn't know how we grew so close so fast, but we did. And I'm not sure when we began ending our phone conversations (even those "chalked up to business") with "I love you."

The first time I heard she had fallen, I was frightened because I realized I had indeed grown to love this wonderful, powerful, assertive friend. I begged her to wear a pendant around her neck that would call emergency personnel if she needed them. After all, she lived alone in a neighborhood that was being bought up by younger, absent families. I worried a lot. But she assured me she would "think about it." It got to where we would laugh each time she said that because we both knew she wouldn't do it but at least she kept me dangling. I would "gently nag" her and she would "think about it" again.

The next time I heard she fell, I was stronger in my pleading. She still did not get the pendant. This time when she fell she spent quite a while "with my head in the hedge" as she said, where she landed after stumbling over some loose concrete in the sidewalk. She later told me a neighbor saw her but "that ninny told me she thought I was looking for a four leaf clover!" We both laughed so hard I wasn't sure if she just made that up.

We've been through a lot together.

On one occasion, we went to her doctor together to see about her diabetes. On several days we had lunch together. One time I sat with her in the hospital while she had a colonoscopy. Afterwards, we made the doctor sit with her and answer all her questions. "I'm so tired of those doctors ignoring me," she would say all too often.

Now, she's getting her house painted. And together we went through the ordeal of her roommate of nine years suddenly moving out overnight. No warning. No good-bye. Nothing. Just an empty room and an unnerving quiet. She found someone to spend an occasional night "because it makes me feel more secure," she confided.

Loneliness crept in although it was never invited. It just walked in and took up space.

However, she is getting through it. She is not getting *over* it, just getting *through* it. That is where the assertiveness, the sense of humor and the smarts come into play. She'll make it. But she shouldn't be alone while she does.

Call your family. They miss you. They want you to ask about them. To really ask.

Where To Find Needed Help?

"Mom has called the police at least a dozen times this month already. It's at the point where the police knock on my door and apologize before I can even say a word," says the weary daughter by way of explanation in a tired, almost robotic voice.

Her mother was a loving, devoted, caring parent. The father was "no longer in the picture," whatever that meant. "She used to love me and take care of me and now she calls the police saying I have locked my only son in the trunk of the car," she related with a cracking voice.

The police know the daughter. But her mother doesn't. Dementia has taken its prisoner. The family can't get her into a facility where she could receive the proper care. She falls through the government cracks, through the financial cracks, through the emotional cracks.

There are no siblings: Just this one daughter, her husband who is about to call it quits over all the problems and a grandson who has to swear continuously to the police that he has never, ever been in the trunk of his mother's car.

Who is there to help?

Legislation is needed to help seniors who don't make enough money but make too much...all at the same time.

Life And Games

He died. He didn't want to. And she didn't want him to.

He was so full of life! Everything was a game. Even when he had to start using a walker he made a game out of it. He was embarrassed to use the darn thing, however. "It makes me look old," he would say. Now, picture this eighty-two-year-old guy and tell me if you think it made him look old.

Fred had red hair. I mean REALLY red hair. Lucille Ball red. Many suspected it was out of a bottle but somehow it suited him. His wife, Sally, would drive him every other Thursday from the eastern shore of Virginia to Richmond, about a two hour drive away, "to get my hair" as he described his favorite barber shop. He would never have it cut anywhere else. He had too much fun driving with Sally and stopping for the forbidden Bar-B-Q sandwich on the way home.

And besides, what would he do about "Johnny Walker?"

This was the game he made up when he realized he absolutely, positively needed an aluminum walker to maneuver. The game went like this… introduce "Johnny" to everyone…and I mean everyone! Then he could get it out of the way and move on to the next fun thing.

They never did have any children. So, he treated the world as if they were his children. Sometimes stern, sometimes forgiving, but always with love and generosity. Oh! Was he generous!

If someone was down in their luck, they would quietly and discretely find a financial answer to their problem. If someone could not afford the entrance fee to their luxury retirement community, it would be quietly, mysteriously written off.

In his honor, Sally funded a large game room at the retirement community for all the residents. She had silent, satisfied tears in her eyes as it was being built.

There was nothing quiet about their love. He would always be laughing and enjoying life. She would always be "pulling up the rear" and buying him toys and trinkets wherever they traveled. They were salt and pepper, always complementing each other but both distinct and flavorful in their very own ways.

But today he died.

The red hair was lying on a white pillow. The suffering was over. The funeral home was spilling over with people. Strange…they were all smiling, chuckling and some even laughing out loud. But of course! Fred and Johnny Walker would have loved this party! We will miss them both.

Life is short. Make every day count. You are giving up a full 24 hours every day to be on this planet. Are you making the most of it?

Stop And Smell The Roses

It was her eighty-first birthday. Elizabeth was giggling and excited and happy. "I made it this far in life," she boasted proudly. Petite, slim and always wearing her twenty-four-inch-long necklace, she was the epitome of being well dressed and coifed. She would have her naturally curly white hair cut every four weeks, without fail.

When I walked into her home to wish her happy birthday, I noticed two lovely vases of flowers. Actually, one was an arrangement of springtime flowers she had placed on the dining room table between two complementing candles in old, tarnished, silver candleholders. Lovely.

The other flower arrangement was in her den in the middle of the coffee table. It was a clear vase overflowing with every imaginable color of rose. "Where did you get those gorgeous roses?" I asked with surprise. Her only answer was a blush that went from her hairline to her collar. She pulled the necklace up to her face in a schoolgirl attempt to hide!

I couldn't believe it; she was holding out on me! She has a boyfriend ("a gentleman caller who I won't give the time of day") she whispered. Even when pressured for further "gossip," she wouldn't answer. The blush continued to dance upon her face.

Then, a smile. The necklace finds its home on her chest. Hair is patted. And we continue as if the question was never asked.

A boyfriend at eighty-one! There is hope for us all!

Love blooms everywhere, every day for everyone. Look for it in the roses.

It's The Little Things

Today was an important day. She had an appointment with her hairdress...at last! It had been over a week and eighty-year-old Mrs. Drake was excited and eager to get out of the house for several reasons.

THIS particular hair appointment was more important than any other. THIS one had to cover up the six stitches in the back of her skull.

She lives a few doors from her professional, doting daughter, Sue, and her family. "Sue was a special surprise," Mom confides behind an age spotted hand held to her mouth. "Her father died two days before she was born; a special person left us and another special person was brought to us." Mother and daughter exchange one of many smiles during our time together.

Living alone in a home that had been in the family for more than fifty years did not prove to be of any concern to Mrs. Drake. Small, tidy and slightly out of style, the home wrapped itself comfortably around this mother of three and one could see how the home and its occupant complemented each other after all these years of taking care of each other.

The same adjectives described the yard: small, tidy and landscape wise, slightly out of date. But never mind. It was home, it was comfortable and it was near family. All good ingredients as one begins to age.

Then she fell.

The six stitches were nasty. She really hurt herself. It was not her first fall but it was by far her worst.

She now needs help. She doesn't want it but realizes staying home alone is no longer an option. With help she won't have to leave and can remain near family. She doesn't want to leave the tidy yard, the small but adequate kitchen, the neighbors, or the car.

She can no longer work in the yard. The kitchen no longer serves her; her daughter does. The neighbors have passed on. And the car sits there "just in case one of the children needs it." But she doesn't want to leave any of it.

Mrs. Drake is sharp, very sharp. She knows what has happened to her way of life and she accepts it; "As long as things remain the same." Does she hear the contradiction? Mini strokes are frequent visitors. Falls are her companions. Her left side is weak, "but improving." The potty chair positions itself next to her bed. And baths are now a once-a-week luxury.

We discuss lots of things. What does it cost to stay in her home? What does it cost to move to a facility that can meet her needs? Does the Veterans Association help widows? Has Meals on Wheels changed their menus? ("My friends say it isn't very tasty.")

Ultimately, the family decides it is better to stay at home for as long as possible. For this family, it should work out. The daughter and her husband have jobs that allow them to be with Mrs. Drake several times a day. A grandson is nearby. Food is brought in and appointments are scheduled by the family who will take her where she needs to go.

Now, who is going to make sure the caregivers don't wear out?

Be careful taking on the responsibility of another person's life. Even when you love that person. Statistically, when it is another full time job on top of your "regular" job, you become the next person who needs help.

Haute Couture And Low Self Esteem

You could hear those spiked heels long before you saw her. Their click, click, click on the lobby's wooden floor was a dead give away in the independent living retirment community. You didn't even have to turn around to know who it was.

She was a contradiction in terms. From those high heels to the top of her head, she was a determined contradiction.

Her high-heeled shoes were elegant, pointed, obviously real leather and expensive. They were a color that would go with anything. Not quite taupe and certainly not beige. She was definitely not a beige person.

Inside the shoes you just knew her toenails had to be polished, perfectly rounded at the corners and would never, ever snag a pair of panty hose.

Her elegant shoes made your eyes appreciate her slim, perfectly shaped legs which rose up into the softest looking chiffon-like dress I have ever seen. Red. Bright, blood red. Defiant red. It was a short skirt, too short except one didn't complain. She had good looking legs and she knew it.

Her hair was cut and shapely but in an out-of-date hairstyle. It was odd to see in a way. Rather like seeing someone from a movie in the 40's step off the movie screen and into your living room to have a conversation you really didn't want to have for some reason. It was a long, sleek pageboy; every platinum blond hair flipped under in perfect precision and uniformity, almost as if it were keeping a forced cadence with her gestapo-like steps in those spiked heels. Both sides of her hair were pulled back and held in place with rhinestone clips; again in perfect placement on each side of her head. Her bangs brought your look to her eyes and finally you see it. What is this "look," this defiance all about?

The tools of expression on her face gave her away. She was trying so desperately. The heels, the legs, the short skirt, the rhinestone hair clips, the youthful hairstyle all faded when you got to her face.

Angry eyes. Squinting, looking for what? Almost like a small, lost animal who knows the larger animal can smell fear so she better put up a good front by being very brave.

A mouth which was perfectly painted to match the red dress was being used to spew anger and insults. Teeth once perfectly shaped and most likely quite attractive were now stained from nicotine and caffeine and were merely used as intruments to help shape the words of fury and defiance.

"This place is for old people, your brochure is all wrong, these prices can't be right, who do you people think you are, why isn't the electricity included, you have got to be kidding!"

These words came tumbling out as if they all held hands and would die if they didn't hold onto each other until heard.

"I'm too young, I wouldn't fit in, the people here are old and I'm not!" More run-on sentences. More anger. She proceeded to point to pictures that were "all wrong," to paint on the wall that was "depressing," to carpet that was "too something... old, I think," she continued to spew.

She was in her seventies and she did not want to be here. Why was she? Finally, she storms out on her taupe stilts and her son and daughter-in-law sit silently until we no longer hear the clicks on the wooden floors and the door slams and the windows shake.

Her son speaks first. With his head bent so that it makes listening difficult, he slowly apologizes for his mother's behavior. He says she lives with he and his wife and it is affecting their marriage. His wife's silent tears are testimony. He loves his mother but had hoped she would "find a friend or something and maybe move out." He confirms that she is also angry at home all the time and they are not sure how much longer they can take it.

In sharp contrast to the way his mother left the room and without another word they slowly rise out of the chairs as if they are seventy year olds. They tenderly take each other's hand as they leave the room and gently, ever so gently pull the door closed.

Growing old can make us furious. Who are we affecting with our fury?

Popping
Hershey Chocolates

"I can tell you the exact moment I started to grow old"!

I couldn't believe my ears. "What do you mean, the exact moment?" "I mean, I know when I was no longer middle aged, when I was suddenly old."

She was silver haired and after all, she was eighty. But to remember the "exact moment?" And with such assuredness?

She sat back in her teal reupholstered chair. She adjusted the foam rubber piece at her back. She had to take the foam everywhere she went since her back operation. It had a hole in the middle of the foam piece where the steel rods that kept her spine straight could rest and not touch the chair. If they did, her pain was excruciating and unbearable. So the foam was her friend and constant companion and sad reminder of not taking enough calcium fifty years ago. This unwanted friend went along on a lot of free rides: operas, plays, dinner parties, bridge games. Like a favorite black dress, it fit comfortably with any occasion. And while she resented its being there, she welcomed its comfort.

The chair was adjusted, the foam found its home in the corner of the chair, and she rested her head back against the headrest. She closed her eyes. For a moment I thought she had fallen asleep. But then a slip of a grin escaped her lips.

Not that one would easily notice because she does not smile a genuine smile very often. But for those of us who know her, it was a smile indeed.

Opening her eyes, she rubbed her arthritic fingers through the naturally curly, soft hair on the back of her head. "It always gets smashed and looks like 'old lady hair', which I hate," she explains. One more chocolate Hershey kiss popped its way into her mouth. Savoring its familiar comfort, she pauses to enjoy the one habit that she has had forever; she's a chocoholic through and through.

Then she proceeds to tell the story through lips that are now not smiling, but are set in her usual matter-of-fact expression. An expression that confirms what she says so often: "I'm here, I guess I might as well enjoy what's left although I don't see much to enjoy anymore."

She began slowly saying, "It was hot outside. So hot that when I drove into the pharmacy's parking lot, I left the windows open so the car would be somewhat bearable when I came out. I always suffer the heat, you know."

How true. Anything hotter than seventy degrees would demand that you better bring a sweater if you're going to visit her because the air conditioning would be groaning in protest from the incessant demands for cold and more cold.

"I was about fifty years old and felt really good in those days."

Those days could be defined as those that were before the emphysema, before the steel rods were placed in her back twice, before her children stopped speaking to each other and before she was even a grandmother and long before she suffered losing her mate of almost fifty years.

She continued saying, "I walked up to the pharmacist to ask a question. As he was responding, I realized I had not stopped sweating but attributed it to the extreme heat and my usual physical response to that kind of environment. The sweat was rolling down my face, it was making itself known on my chest as it darkened my purple T-shirt between my breasts and made the back of the shirt cling to me like sticky fly paper.

"So I took out a tissue and started to discreetly, or so I thought, dab at my face to try to mop up a torrent of water that came out of nowhere. I was on my third tissue when I left the store.

When I gratefully slipped into my cold oasis in the air-conditioned car, I adjusted the mirror before backing up. Only then did I notice spots on my face where I had dabbed to absorb the excess water. I had left small, extremely obvious pieces of tissue! I must have had a hundred specks of tissue on my face. From my hairline to my chin and down my throat I looked like I had been shot with a BB gun full of hand cream making little white mounds on my face!

"I was stunned at first as I tried to figure out what I was seeing. Then when I realized what it was, a giggle started down in my stomach and rose with a roar of laughter as I imagined what the pharmacist was thinking! I realized he kept a straight face the whole time I was talking to him. But it does explain his assistant who kept coming by and smiling, smiling and smiling some more each time she passed. Now, I understand. I was the sideshow. And that was when I <u>knew</u>. I was in menopause and I was old."

Old age can strike at different times.

Two Peas In A Pod, Sort Of

They were sisters. Not exactly two peas in a pod, more like two vegetables on the same plate. You know the kind of vegetables we see on our plates as kids. Different and never ever touching. We eat one completely and then the other just as completely. But never, not ever, do we eat them together.

One sister was more like a soft, sweet, lumpy pile of veggies. It sits quietly where it is supposed to sit on the plate. The other sister was like a rigid vegetable, hard to chew and obviously tough on the digestive system. Very different from each other but sisters, nonetheless.

One wanted an apartment with a view in the retirement community. The other one wanted to stay in her independent living condo on the beach and "never leave until they carry me out horizontal," she emphatically stated while shaking her finger at anyone who would listen.

Neither wanted to be dependent on the other. It's funny. They couldn't see how they were already very, very dependent on each other. Neither one had much money. Neither one had any children. And neither one wanted to grow old. "But here we are; two old ninnies," said the older one. The younger one snorted, turned her head and pretended to look out the window at nothing.

One drove to the grocery store on Tuesdays, the other ran the errands on Thursdays and both of them pestered their rich bachelor brother for money every weekend when he would come over for some "home cooking."

"Why are we here? We can't afford this place. There are too many old people living here. Why did I agree to come here with you today?" The younger sister was whining and grousing and picking at the luncheon they were enjoying at the open house hosted by the local retirement community.

The rigid, hard to digest one was quite obviously tired of explaining this over and over. She first stared at her sister. Then she picked up her fork, changed her mind and put it down, took a drink of sweetened tea and seemed to contemplate the lemon precariously hanging over the edge of her glass.

Slowly she said, "We are here because I have cancer and no one to take care of me."

We fell silent. We didn't know where to look as we picked at our suddenly warm chicken salad and Jell-O.

They walked out. The rigid one not quite as straight and the soft one shuffling along with a take-out doggie bag.

Later that month I read where the rigid one had died alone in her independent condo overlooking the beach.

Where do we go when we are sick and have no one to care for us?

Making Decisions With Silk Scarves

They were sitting in the audience, not too close to the speaker but not in the back, either. I was giving a presentation about the choices of local retirement communities. She was paying close attention. The silk scarf around her throat hinted at a reason for their being there.

Her companion was tall and obviously retired military. Close-cropped, black hair, slim build, and strong handshake, with the posture of a general reviewing the troops. Only he smiled a lot. Just a soft smile that didn't seem to fit his face. At first he seemed to be there as a reluctant listener, the kind of reluctance you see on a child's face

107

when they're made to visit their great aunt who they hardly know and who smells funny anyway. But there he was listening, even if it was out of politeness. I thought he was such a kind son to accompany his mother to this presentation. I was sure he had better things to do with his time.

She, on the other hand, was extremely attentive. She most especially wanted to know how to approach her children about her decision to make this move. I thought even more of her son. She must be asking him to accompany her so it will be easier to talk to the other children later on.

I could understand.

After all, she had that attractive, silk scarf around her neck that did not even try to hide the artificial voice box but simply tried to make her feel more feminine. It was working. It did its job.

She asked a few questions that helped me understand that being independent was paramount on her mind. She wanted to find a place to live where she "wouldn't be a burden."

She had survived her throat cancer. She had made friends with her new voice. And the hump in her back was testimony to an obvious case of osteoporosis. Her slight build, bruised arms and caved in facial features were opening chapters to what must be a story of eating little and falling often.

More questions, more answers and like reading a book backwards...the last chapter first... we laughed as we formally introduced ourselves after we had been talking for almost fifteen minutes.

That's when I was introduced to her black-haired, perfect-postured, slim-built, HUSBAND.

Disease can rob us of health and beauty. But those who truly love us see us from the inside more than the outside.

Rogue Pilot Wearing Blue Pajamas

The sun was bright in his sterile hospital room. He was lying in bed, eyes closed, wearing clean pajamas and freshly shaved. They were new pajamas, the kind that still have the crease from the folds made by the package, deep blue with white piping around the one breast pocket. His chin was sporting a white little speck. A tissue was there to catch the trickle of blood made by the small nick from the razor and it was peaked like a tiny coolie hat. He was never one to greet people with much exuberance, so I had not planned to disturb him. I just wanted to sit next to him and I guess I hadn't planned to do anything. He was not the kind of man you planned to "do" with; he just "was."

But he opened his eyes; they were so blue. With his cleft chin sporting that small fresh shaving nick, he was nevertheless still quite the looker. I always saw him as so very handsome. I could see what the women of his time must have seen in him at first glance…those blue eyes. They are steel blue, not a soft blue. But steel has its place. It supports, it's dependable and always there, it holds things up and together, it's strong.

Steel is not soft, not gentle and it doesn't know how to hug. But it is always reliable. He is so reliable and strong but he can't hug.

Blue eyes open and crinkle around the edges. White lines at the corners where he's always squinting in the sun. His skin is always dark in the summer. They say he has Indian blood. Who knows? He never did talk much about himself.

For some reason, he starts to talks to me, really talk. He talks about how he's feeling, "better"; talks about the service in the hospital, "pretty good"; talks about the food, "oh, you know." Not an in-depth conversation but conversation nonetheless and with me, only me! Like an occasional drip that continues until it is a steady stream, a thought slowly occurs to me. For fifty years we have never had a complete conversation, just the two of us. Oh, we skirted around topics like two ice skaters enjoying the rink but never holding hands to help each other.

I can't even remember what we discussed. I can only remember that we talked and talked. A conversation that went back and forth, back and forth, as it's supposed to between two people. He actually smiled. He actually wanted to hear what I was saying. I had tears in my eyes that I attributed to the bright sun.

Then he stopped. I looked up to see what had caused this abrupt change. His wife had walked in.

His eyes closed. He rested his head on the sterile pillowcase monogrammed with the black hospital crest. He turned his head toward the sun and metamorphosed into the man I knew all these years...quiet, introspective.

Then she began to talk. All conversation was hers. All attention was to her. He never opened his eyes again that evening. And we never had another conversation between just the two of us.

Watching this scene play itself out, I recalled one of the few stories he shared about his teenage youth. I could see him in my mind's eye as a young man. He told of lying on his back in the rumble seat of the model A Ford, knees bent and supporting a propped gun and aimed straight up in the air. The driver, another teenager, drove the car while my eighteen-year-old father took aim at every lamp post as they slowly and methodically drove under each one.

I'm not sure why this image came to me as I watched him on the hospital bed, his breath becoming more and more shallow. I never knew what "shallow breath" meant until I watched it myself. Each breath HAD to be his last. I did not believe anyone could live breathing so few breaths.

Finally his last one came and went. Nothing was left.

The World War II pilot was gone. His Distinguished Flying Cross Medal would be awarded once more after his death. Only this time it went to the wife's most favored child and would insert one more splinter in an already fractured family of numerous, un-favored children.

He had chosen his death. The idea of diapers on this rogue pilot, hospital beds in his living room and women having to spoon feed him, helped him make up his mind. He left rather than submit to what he called "that humiliation."

As his eyelids closed on those beautiful blue eyes for the last time, his grandson abruptly turned toward the window. Later the grandson said he was hoping to get a glimpse of his grandfather's soul as he took to the skies again.

Never underestimate the power of the mind and the body even at our most vulnerable times.

Buckingham Palace Revisited

My car pulls up to a very neat, 1950's ranch style home with a tidy yard and cleanly swept carport housing a twenty-three-year-old car that is just as tidy as the rest of the place. A daughter greets me at the door with a worried look on her face.

Not surprisingly, the interior of the home is neat. Magazines about fishing, boating and the latest AARP edition are neatly stacked on a coffee table that smells of fresh furniture polish.

A true Southern gentleman, seated in his favorite beige but worn armchair, rises to greet me with the words, "See, I can get up by myself." Getting out of the recliner alone was an accomplishment each day of his eighty-plus-year-old life. At first glance, it doesn't look as if it would be much of an accomplishment at all for such a slight man. He is smaller than his 5'6" daughter. He probably doesn't weigh 135 pounds. But I can see and hear his fear. He is afraid if he can't get out of the chair by himself EVERY DAY he will have to go to "the home."

What a sweetie. He has a smile that lights up the room and probably the neighborhood judging from the neighbors who enjoy checking on him daily. They all love to check on Al. Why not? He is charming, witty, and always has a bowl of chocolate candy waiting for the visitor. Not just any chocolate. He has Dove chocolate. This guy knows what he's doing!

A slightly built man, he wears a sweater in the summer. He doesn't seem to have enough of his own padding to keep warm. And he's not eating properly and he's lonely. Even daily visits from kind neighbors aren't enough for this little elf of a man. Since his wife died a few years ago, he hasn't gone dancing. He loved to dance! And he eats out for every meal…EVERY meal. And now his daughter has to write the checks to pay his bills, "but I sign them," he assures me.

As we sit down to chat and see how I can be of assistance, I'm totally enveloped by him. His smile takes me in and charms me before I realize what has hit me. And he immediately invites me back in time to WWII.

"If I have to move and go a*nywhere*, I'm taking that picture," he announces to his daughter and me. I don't blame him. Following the direction he is pointing to with his slightly gnarled, arthritic index finger, I turn my gaze from the large picture window that overlooks a basin of tidal water and nesting gray herons, to see a yellowing, framed picture of two young men standing in front of Buckingham Palace in England. They couldn't be over twenty-one-years old. Both are leaning against a black, iron gate. Both have one leg cocked in front of the other and arms are folded across the chest of their freshly laundered military uniforms while their smiles take up the entire photo. It's Al! It has to be!

Sure enough, it is. That smile that bewitched me across a dining room table comes at me again from the photo on the dining room wall. "I bet you were a whole lot of trouble in your youth," I declared. His smile widens and becomes a deep cavern where a belly laugh enjoys living and spills out into the room for all of us to enjoy. "Boy! You don't know the half!" he responds. His daughter raises her eyebrows and we laugh even harder.

He misses his wife. He misses their meals together. The "nice people" at the local diner don't make up for her absence. He misses their dancing. His driving is erratic and a little scary and he knows it. He misses the card games they used to play. And he misses being able to work in his tidy yard.

However, he still has that smile. While it hides from time to time as we talk about alternative living options, it always seems to find its place again under those mischievous eyes.

He works his way back to the worn recliner. His head gently hits the familiar place on the headrest and his fingers curl around the end of the arms as old friends greeting each other. He doesn't rise as I leave nor as the herons take flight from their nest. His mischievous eyes miss the graceful take off of the birds and he begins to snooze.

As he drifts off (maybe mentally slipping into the military uniform again and getting into more youthful trouble) he mumbles ever so softly, "When I REALLY can't take care of myself, I might give some thought to moving. Zzzzzz."

Who know best when it is time to make "the" move?

Dance The Night Away.

I'm quite sure she could never reach as high as an ice-maker in the top freezer of a refrigerator. There is no way! She is so small! Her tiny frame is crowned with bouncing, white hair that not only bounces but also seems to jiggle. Can hair jiggle? Hers does. Curls that obviously have crowned her head since infancy seem at home dancing on her head as if to some invisible orchestra only they can hear.

At first the white crown of curls does a slow waltz as she approaches me. Then as she gets closer and more animated in her step, her hair does a quick two-step. Her locks go into full throttle as she gets excited with what she is about to tell me. Finally the dance ends with a solo jig all over her head! Curls bouncing, springing, falling excitedly over her eyebrows only to be pulled back by the invisible dance partner to take another step. What motion!

It is only enhanced by the excitement in her eyes. She can't wait to tell me what she did last night. She went dancing! She goes quite frequently. "But last night was different," she explains. How so? Did she buy a new dress? New shoes? Find a new dance club?

Her excitement was about a man! And so was her dilemma. It seems that *her* being ninety-five-years-old (impossible!) and *his* being seventy-five-years-old was a problem. "Honey," she said,

"I just don't feel right robbing the cradle!" You go, girl!

Age is only a state of mind

To Move Or Not To Move?

As I drive into the expensive neighborhood, I notice almost all the homes are large, expansive, with massive lawns sloping into a beautiful body of water. All this beauty obviously takes a great deal of money and time to maintain.

Fumbling with the piece of paper that contains the address, I finally find the home where I'm to meet the family. I walk across an overgrown, neglected lawn, so very obviously out of place in this neighborhood. It is hard to miss the curtains that are faded and split from the sun at the front windows or the leaves matted down in the corners of the front porch. The front door needs repairing and paint. Obviously, no one has been out the front door in a long time. And I'm sure the neighbors wish someone would!

I'm greeted at the door by a devoted great-niece who is trying to work and take care of a childless great-aunt who is almost ninety-years old and now lives alone.

Aunt Lulu just lost her husband of sixty years. She has round-the-clock help since he passed away. Julie, the great-niece, is sure he passed away from the responsibility of taking care of "his bride." That's what he called her even after all those years. They were like two lovebirds. He still opened the car door for her and still helped her into her chair when they sat down to eat the meals he faithfully prepared.

He was quite famous in his line of work. As a consequence, they traveled the world, several times over. Never having any children, they were devoted totally and completely to each other.

Then he died.

Aunt Lulu found herself totally without direction. He was her mate, her chef, her driver, and even her doctor from time to time. She trusted him more than anyone else. How could he leave her? Why did he do it?

Her forgetful mind could not accept or understand any of these events.

Her family wants Aunt Lulu to move to an assisted living community. "But why," she asks continuously? "I'm doing fine where I am." The great-niece turns to me for help, advice and, I think, also as a sounding board.

Julie is President of a large printing company and has TWO children of her own (one of who was recently diagnosed with severe depression and was failing college). Her husband understands but he's getting tired of Julie always being at her great-aunt's home and never home with him. "The sad thing is," Julie laments, "he's right. I'm at my great-aunt's home more than my own, and my family and business are falling apart because of it."

Ultimately, we sat down with Aunt Lulu and showed her how much it was costing her to stay at home with full time help ("I hate those people, anyway," she confessed in a small whisper.) We compared that to what it would cost her to move to a retirement community. Although it took her several months to think it all through and to get over the fear of change, she was able to make the decision to "try it for a while." She didn't sell her home at once "just in case," but it ended up a happy story. She really liked it! She could continue writing her short stories, watch her soaps with friends, enjoy meals with her new acquaintances and when she was tired, she retreated to her beautiful room. It was a difficult decision but the right one for everyone.

Sometimes making the move, even when it's difficult, is the right move.

Interlaced But Independent Laces

The caller is an angry daughter. As the only child of an eighty-year-old mother, Sally is at her wits end.

"Mother's so negative - all the time! And she thinks that we have nothing else to do except wait on her, hand and foot! She won't even try." The tears from no sleep, anger, frustration, fear, and anxiety build up in her dark brown eyes until the dam breaks. She sobs so hard I can't help but wonder when was the last time she allowed herself to cry. She is exhausted.

Sally has a professional career, two small children, beautiful tow-headed little girls, two and four years old. They are miniature versions of their daddy. Dad is an engineer who graduated from a top Ivy League University. He is used to logic - things that fit squarely in a box. And he's having a hard time understanding his mother-in-law. I see and hear his frustration and it is quite apparent that it is putting a strain on this young family.

Actually, Sally looks more like she should be her mother's granddaughter. I estimate her to be in her mid thirties and her mother is almost eighty. Sally's father has been dead for many years. I don't dare ask, but I wonder if she's adopted. She doesn't look anything like her mother; their mannerisms, eye color, build, hands, skin tone, voice...nothing at all ties them together. They remind me of two shoelaces that are holding a foot in a shoe. Only one shoelace is long, white, with the tips of the laces wrapped in plastic and they make a nice bow. The other shoelace is brown or tweed, short and frayed and looks like it should be wrapped around a package ready to mail. Both are doing the same job and on the same shoe, but absolutely everything says they don't belong together.

Sally's mother, Thelma, is lying on the bed at the nursing home. She has been "kicked out again from two other nursing homes," according to Sally. "She gets our attention by feigning illness. If I have plans to go on a trip, she calls the hour we are supposed to leave. If we don't call often enough, she calls 911. And we are over there every night! What else can we do?"

The doctors have diagnosed her mother with "failure to thrive". She also has emphysema and other pulmonary diseases. She weighs less than eighty-five pounds. She won't eat. She won't get out of bed and she's hooked up to her hissing companion, oxygen, twenty-four hours a day. Large blue veins march along her elongated fingers. These veins look like a pathway for a small army that marches to nowhere. Over knuckle hills, around wrist corners, up the thumb and back down to the inside wrist.

Her hair parts down the back of her head from lying hours on end in the bed. The bed is hard. She complains about it but the family has stopped listening. The nurses don't respond as quickly because she calls and calls and calls…day after day after day.

"My bed is hard. The food is bad. Where is my medicine? You aren't my nurse, who are you? Where are my clothes? Those aren't my clothes. When am I going home? I can't go home alone. You don't need to know how much is in my checking account. Don't bring the grandchildren here, they make too much noise. I don't know what I did with the money from the bank! I can't eat! I'm hungry. Why don't you bring me anything to eat? You know I hate the food here. I told you years ago you should never have married that guy. There are only old people here. Why am I here? Why isn't your father visiting me? What do you mean he's dead? That's crazy. You're crazy! He was just here visiting with me."

The endless stream of questions, demands, accusations. Crying, begging, pleading. Anger, insults, silent treatments. Exhaustion.

The family has been dealing with this for over two years. They are drained. They need help, understanding and compassion. And Sally's mother needs release.

The aging process can be accepted or rejected. Either way, it comes – ready or not.

Becoming A Statistic

The abuse was subtle. It was not anything the family could detect. No bruises, no marks of any kind, for that matter, at least not on her body. But the caregiver started shoving and pushing. She began to throw things to the patient instead of handing them to her. She stopped answering the midnight calls for assistance. Fear set in with the patient and then pain set in. The patient became a statistic.

She is at least eighty-five years old. She doesn't have an actual birth certificate but that is a close guess. She has slight memory problems but the world's sweetest smile makes up for any lack of memory. And those pearls! She wears a string of pearls with everything! They aren't real ones, just happy ones. White and elegant, they lay against her soft chest as a badge given for her years, a badge she wears proudly.

"How could I have known?" moaned the daughter? "What did I do wrong? What could I have done differently? Why didn't I notice?"

While taking her mother to the doctor, the daughter found her usually lively parent quiet, sullen and not responsive. At a stop sign, the daughter took her mother's hand and that gesture of love and care opened the dam of tears held back so valiantly in her mother's eyes.

"I don't want to go back home!" she wailed. The startled daughter pulled the car off the road and gently scooped up her mom into her arms.

Her mother's home had represented everything to this sweet, gentle senior - security, comfort, memories, love. And she had always resisted any suggestion of moving to an alternative living community. Now, her once comforting home held the threat of abuse.

"She hurt me and she's mean." Her mother spoke in a whimper. The daughter's heart was at first uncomprehending, then denying, then furious as comprehension took hold.

The daughter called me and could barely speak. Her voice was that of an excited, frightened child – high pitched, rapid, words falling into each other so that they lost their meaning. They had no meaning except for extreme anger. "Help me get that woman out of my mother's home!"

The caregiver left, the company did not apologize and mom moved into a loving assisted living community. She didn't want to make the move, but a new, incomprehensible feeling had invaded her life – a feeling of fear.

Are we not only listening to our seniors but also observing any changes in their lives?

Thanks, Pal

The November air was exhilarating. My husband and I were taking a late afternoon walk when we noticed her. Wearing a sweater against the cool weather, she had her head bent down and her eyes focused on her feet. Each sweater-wrapped arm held a bundle. Each bundle obscured her vision of her feet. And her right arthritic hand was doing its best to hold onto a clunky, wooden banister as she attempted to go up two flights of stairs. The stairs were an obstacle in themselves. They were two flights up, made of thick, wooden planks meant to withstand the elements. But numerous nails were popping up as the years weathered them so that the stairs were no longer a convenient means of getting upstairs, they were a barrier to slow-moving feet and poor vision.

She had each foot firmly but gently planted on an equally clunky wooden step, not the same step, but gingerly on two different steps. She was balanced for the moment. But she was almost frozen in her position. I sensed she was not afraid, but that something was not right.

Watching her made me so nervous! I couldn't help myself. I called out confessing honestly, "You are making me nervous; may I help you?"

Laughing eyes looked up to greet me with a beautiful smile. Giggling, the gray haired great-grandmother was almost embarrassed. She didn't even respond. She continued to giggle and we started laughing with her. Only then could I see she wasn't in any danger of falling, quite the contrary. She was so balanced with packages, sweaters, feet, and handrails, that she didn't dare "unbalance" herself.

We approached her and with a gentle smile she invited my husband to take her arm as I took her packages. We all ascended the next two flights of stairs together. When we reached the top, we opened her door and helped her in.

She thanked us profusely saying, "I hope one day when you are eighty-seven years old, someone helps you, too. Thanks, pal." Her gift to us was a pat on the arm, a twinkle in her eye, a smile that everyone loves when they see it on their grandmother's face and off she went. I suppose she was going to make a nice meal with all those goodies she was carrying up the stairs. Part of me wanted to sit down and talk to her. She was so inviting and grateful. But something told me she was going to be fine. So we said good-bye to our new "pal" and resumed our walk.

Who is going to be there for us when we are eighty-seven years old and need a little help up the stairs?

The Neglected Adult Child

The corners of her mouth were turned up. The face muscles were attempting to make a smile. In a way, they were successful. The lips were in that mode, turned up at the corners, slightly parted and in place. But it wasn't real. It wasn't authentic or genuine. It was perfunctory. The smile was there because it had to be, it was expected.

It was her eyes, that conduit to our real feelings, that gave her away. They did not belong with that attempt of a smile. They were silently screaming. Loud and clear, they expressed fear, distrust, confusion and some anger.

Her daughter had asked me over to their home. "Mom is so mean. She always has been." The catch in her throat and the unshed tears were on the surface of her quivering voice. It was obvious these were old feelings the daughter was expressing. Along with the catch was a sigh, a reluctant acceptance of what she could not control but neither could she accept. "She has always been so mean to me, even when I was a child, and now that she is older and has dementia I'm at such a loss. How do I help someone who never helped me? How do I become the daughter that she needs but that I don't know how to be - that I can't be?" The tears burn red-hot, her cheeks glow with fierce frustration and her fists ball up only to stack themselves one on the other. I have the feeling that she would give almost anything to put one or both of those fists right through the wall.

The daughter, the only child of this widow, works full time and has a husband and a family of her own. She has always been on the edge of her mother's life. Not really invited in. So as a result, she was always on the outside. She found it to be a comfortable place to be, actually. They never were close. When her father died any family ties and love seemed to die with him. But, "She is my mother, after all, and I know I should do something, but I don't know how or what that should be."

So, she hired a personal friend, Anne, to be her mother's care -provider. It has been working for two years. But for the last few weeks, all of the sudden, when left alone, her mother is becoming worse.

She smokes. She plays with matches. She won't eat. She calls her brother for cigarettes in the middle of the night if Anne quietly hides them. She opens the garage door at all hours and forgets why. She roams the house looking for car keys that have long been taken away. Food is put in the microwave only to be forgotten.

We talk about mom moving to a community that can take care of her. And the daughter cries as only a daughter can.

No matter our age, we are always the child when the parent is in need. How sad when the adult child was neglected.

Love Will Overpower Fear Everytime.

I was having a difficult time concentrating. After all, the family had invited me into their home to discuss some serious matters. The family was warm and comfortable. Just like the lemon tea that was steeping in the old fashioned, towel-covered cozy. Outside, the snow was falling in huge, gigantic flakes that invited the child in me to quickly run out with my face to the sky and to stick out my tongue to try to catch the cold offerings from the over-cast clouds.

Four ducks were swimming military-style, one precisely after the other in the freezing lake outside the window. How could they stand the cold, I wondered. And how did they choose who would be the leader?

The white snowflakes were such a contrast to the dark feathers of the ducks. Surely this was where the great artists received their inspiration - from Gods' creatures and landscapes. As a gray heron swooped in with the grace of a ballerina dancing on down feathers, and made a soft landing near the bank of the still lake, I had to pull myself back to reality.

What the family really needed was someone to bounce ideas off of so they could make sense of their concerns.

The daughter, young but wise, had called saying her mother was beginning to "show signs of aging and forgetfulness." Could we talk? All of us, together?

The daughter and her husband met me at the door of their colonial style home. The house and the softly falling snow seemed to be out of a Norman Rockwell painting. I could almost hear the house sigh with contentment.

Mom was watching the snow fall outside a bay window where we all joined together at the family table. Tea was offered and accepted. Comfort set in.

But Mom was nervous. She lived three states away from both of her daughters and she was here on a short visit. Her friends were dying. Her memory "wasn't what it used to be," and she knew it. Fear was once again an unwelcome visitor. Will He stay for good this time?

Never before had I seen a daughter able to put her mother so at ease. "Mom," she said, "we don't want anything to change. We just want to know what to do if a change in your life presents itself. We're afraid of not doing what is right for you if a change does occur. So we want to hear what the consultant has to say and what you think. We will do whatever you want. We love you very much."

One silent tear fell from Mom's eye. Her arthritic fingers clasped and unclasped a tissue. I reached over and put my hand over hers and said, "You are very, very lucky. Some parents have children who wait until there is a disaster and then do what's convenient for them, not the parent."

Mom looked up at me for what seemed like a long time. I guess she was looking into my eyes to see if I were telling the truth. And she believed.

She squeezed my hand, dabbed at her eyes, smiled and took a sip of tea. We began to talk.

Fear of the unknown can become acceptance when love steps in.

Second Marriage: Older Man

He was just standing there. He was doing the "husband wait" stand. You know the kind - looking a little out of place, both hands in his trouser pockets because he didn't know what to do with them. He was very handsome. White hair and deep blue, flashing eyes. His white hair was really more yellow-white, hinting at a blond youth. I had to stand in line next to him and as I approached, he smiled a warm smile that reached up to his happy eyes. This was a contented man. He also looked like a CEO terribly out of place, as if someone should be standing in line in his stead. It turned out I was right on all accounts.

I wasn't aware of it then, but I knew his wife. Upon learning that news after some idle chitchat, his comfort level with life became clear. A few years previous, he had married for the second time. "This time it's right," he recited easily. Not being much of a talker, this was a pretty long sentence for George.

He wife soon finished her retail business and joined us. We hugged as friends do when they have not seen each other in a long time. She glowed also. She had married a man sixteen years her senior, she had a thriving real estate business, her children were grown up and successful and grandchildren were on the way. Today they were getting ready to take their yacht out for a weeklong cruise along the Potomac River. Life was good.

We lost touch again. Why do we let that happen? Someone wonderful comes back into your life and you let that thread to a comfortable friend once again slip through your busy fingers.

This time when she called things were different. It had been several years and George now had Alzheimer's disease. "He just sits at the computer, he works his cross-word puzzles and he stares into space," she lamented. Then came the diagnosis of his lung cancer. He was cognizant enough to know what that meant. "I hope they collide together on the same day and I can check out," he joked about both diseases. The joke fell on deaf, angry ears.

We talked about how she had to take care of herself as well as take care of him. She asked in a voice barely above a whisper, "What does that mean - take care of myself?"

I asked her if she was beginning to stay home because it was "easier," to eat whatever was convenient? Had she stopped seeing her friends; did she cry a lot when she was alone? Her silence confirmed everything.

"He doesn't want me to go out. I feel so guilty. He gets so angry over nothing at all." The sentences spilled over themselves trying to get out. But no tears fell. She was either holding them in or there were no more to shed.

"This was just not what I expected when I was thirty-nine years old marrying a handsome, successful older man. "How," she asked, "did this happen?"

How do we prepare for the future when the future is unthinkable?

Content In Boxer Shorts And T-shirts

He walked into the room in his sox and boxer shorts and a T-shirt. He looked confused but happy to see his wife – twenty-five years his junior. A maid gently guided him into his bedroom where he made himself more socially presentable.

"So, how are you, my dear?" Mr. Charm asked as he returned to the living room where I sat with his wife. He extended his hand to shake mine. He had a powerful grip and he looked me straight in the eye. He had alert blue eyes and he now sported crisp, professional-looking slacks and a pin-stripped shirt that he was casually buttoning at the wrist. He looked like the executive he was for almost forty years. That was before the Alzheimer's became a part of his life.

With his tiny dog in his lap, we had a wonderful conversation for ten minutes. Then he couldn't remember the name of his dog or the dog's age. He couldn't remember what to call the room where we sat. But could he reminisce about how he met his wife. He remembered what she wore, where they were and all the circumstances. Their eyes met, they exchanged a private, unspoken moment as only two lovers can do and then he asked why he was wearing his sweater. "You were going to take out the dog, dear." "Oh, yes…that's right… the dog. What's his name?"

He left to step into the front yard with the small ball of fur that had been his constant companion for more than a year now. We watched to make sure they both came back in.

As he hung up his sweater, his wife said, "He's starting to eat with his fingers when we go out with friends." Sighing, she looked back out the window and I saw from her slumped shoulders that she already missed what they once had.

Enjoy every minute of every day.

Emphysema Demons Under The Bed

In my minds eye I pictured the demon smiling as she told her story. You know the smile. The one you remember as a child. The smiling monster under the bed waiting for you to put one foot off onto the cold bedroom floor where the demon would gleefully grab you by the ankle and drag you kicking and screaming under the bed to his domain - never to be seen by your parents again.

It was that demon smile I envisioned as I imagined her inhaling from her inhaler, trying to fend off the emphysema demon again.

It started out the usual way. The daughter knocked on the apartment door of the high-end

senior community. She didn't expect her mother
to be able to walk to the door to open it for her but
she knocked nonetheless as she slowly opened the
door. Sure enough the mother was sitting in her
usual place in her favorite living room chair. The
cat was lying in his usual place - at the foot of her
favorite living room chair.

The daughter made the usual comment: "You
are going to kill yourself trying to step over that
cat one day." The mother made the usual clucking
noises and ignored her, as always.

Putting on her vest to go shopping was an
exercise in patience and exasperation on both their
parts. "It's hard to see these tiny zippers," said the
mother. "They don't make them any smaller than
they used to," said the daughter. Both women
grunted at the comment of the other.

Taking their time to walk to the elevator, out the building and to the car, the mother and daughter, with twin strides, struggled with the trunk where the daughter placed the mother's wheelchair and oxygen tank inside.

"Mother, if you get one more disease, you won't be able to fit it into your car." They chuckled at the irony and sadness of the statement.

It was tiring, frustrating, exasperating and time consuming to take her mother out to the mall. But the mother was lonely and had cabin fever from a sudden winter storm and they both needed to get out.

When they reached the mall, the usual wheelchair dance began again.

Get out the handicapped sticker.

Take the oxygen clip off her nose while in the car.

Get the pillow for her back to put in the wheelchair.

Open the trunk.

Get out the wheelchair.

"Did you get the part for my feet? You forgot them last time, you know."

"Yes, mother." (Did she ever forget?)

Put the foot pedals on the damn thing.

Place the pillow in correctly.

Ease her into the wheelchair.

Hook up the portable oxygen.

Purse in the lap.

Whew!

Into the mall they went.

What the daughter saw was utterly amazing. Everywhere they went the people were kind, gentle, helpful, and even generous.

The sales lady came from around the counter with a clipboard and knelt down so the mother could sign for her purchases from her wheelchair.

The burly motorcycle-gang-looking-member held open the door and wished her a good day.

The pharmacist gave her a discount "because you're so good looking," he teased. The mother and daughter giggled like two young girls.

The waiter gave her an extra portion and "threw in" a small dessert when he realized she was taking home the leftovers for her dinner tomorrow night when she will be eating alone – again – because she didn't want to "stand out" in the retirement community dining room carrying the oxygen tank she constantly needed.

Everywhere around them were people who used her as a reason to be thoughtful. They encouraged their little children to pick up her packages. They reminded their reluctant teenage sons to open a door. Or she gave them an excuse to smile or pat her hand.

Amazing.

After a while both women were ready to go home.

The inhaler made another appearance and the dance began again with the wheelchair taking the lead.

Being alone is not the same as being lonely.

Poster Child

I think his smile could have opened the door by itself. It seemed to have a life of it's own with snow-white teeth below sparkling blue eyes. Its owner could be the poster child for the expression "grinning from ear to ear."

A warm handshake, a slight bow from the waist, and a gracious sweeping of the hand that guided me to the only semi-available chair in the room that consisted of six chairs and two sofas. How very odd. Every surface of every piece of furniture was covered with knick-knacks, books, odd gloves, old empty purses, stacks of papers, a turned-over vase devoid of any flowers. One Victorian- style chair had its dark velour covering spotted with what must have been a very old stain of curious origin.

Another ancient settee was a menagerie for small stuffed animals - lions, cats, dogs, whales, bears, seals. Many of them were without various parts of their bodies or lacking in stuffing. "They belong to Shotzie," said the senior "poster child." At the mention of his name, a black mongrel of a dog, equally ill-kept but obviously well-loved, thumped his tail on one of the few barren parts of the cluttered wooden floor. Shotzie then took that as his cue to jump up on the settee to rummage through his zoo to find the most appropriate offering. Upon being chosen, the one-eyed, one-eared, three-legged gift was plopped at the visitor's feet. The tail thumping began again. You could almost see the grin on the dog's face.

I could swear he was thinking, "Do ya like it? Huh? Huh? Do ya?"

Shotzie's owner perched on the edge of a rickety chair. It wasn't easy. His two new, bionic knees plus the undiagnosed stiffness in his back made easing into the chair a precarious and almost frightening event. Sweat broke out on his forehead. And the chair groaned at its new load.

Grimacing with obvious pain, he lowered himself into the old chair. Finally settled, the senior's smile reappeared on his face.

Earlier in the week, he had placed a call for assistance about some senior concerns. I emphasize HE had called for help. He was almost ninety years old. His wife was even older. But she didn't believe they needed any help. He believed they needed lots of it. He was right.

Their blended-family children were scattered around the country and even though they were concerned, they couldn't help except as the occasional holiday or vacation allowed them.

He wanted help with meals and finding a new doctor. "My current doctor treats me like I'm stupid," he groused. They needed a housekeeper, a yardman and someone to manage their numerous medications. "I'm not sure what I should be taking anymore," he confessed. And the bills were not getting paid because his wife refused to relinquish the checkbook to him.

She refused everything. "We are just fine," she sniffed. The fact that she was almost completely deaf, had partial vision in only one eye, and walked with a walker over more scatter rugs than could be counted, did not seem to be of concern to her. HE was concerned, however.

Last week she fell. The week before he fell. And just yesterday, they BOTH fell - together! While neither one broke anything, they remained on the kitchen floor until a neighbor happened to come by.

"We are just fine," she reiterated as he told me of their numerous falls and near falls.

After much conversation and eye rolling and head shaking on his wife's part, he gratefully took the information of resources and services who would be able to assist them in their home. Because his wife refused to move to an alternative living community, he was tethered to poor meals, a hard-to-maintain home, unpaid bills, poor hygiene and isolation.

I left them with a heavy heart.

Shouldn't both partners make life decisions?

Favorite Cereals And Fat Free Yogurt

She did not plan on being a widow. No one ever does. But being a *young* widow was never, ever in her thoughts.

She knew she was a "young senior." She was barely over fifty-five and he had just celebrated his sixtieth birthday. She sighed to herself as she stared out at the ocean in front of her. "It's still so very unfair; we had our whole lives ahead of us," she shared with the ocean.

As next-door neighbors, we had started talking over the fence and decided to take an impromptu walk when she began to reminisce and share her thoughts.

She and her husband had been on their daily bike ride on the boardwalk. They were both trying to lose weight (he needed to, she didn't). Both had dropped their cholesterol levels and he could notch his belt one more hole. They were going to celebrate by biking to the yogurt store a few blocks away and indulge in a cup of fat-free yogurt. They were still discussing how they were going to do that. He only liked vanilla and she only liked chocolate. A dilemma they took great delight in solving!

In mid-sentence, he fell off the bike, almost as if he were laying down the bike instead of falling off of it. She thought he must have hit a rock or blown a tire. But no, he had died.

Memories came back in slow motion now. It had been almost a year and while she could talk about it a little easier, it was painfully obvious that reality had not found a home with her yet.

We resumed our walk and she lamented that she had to do some long overdue housekeeping. She asked, "If I throw away his favorite cereal box does it mean that he isn't coming back?" It was difficult to tell if she was asking me, herself or the ocean. No one answered.

Plan and play as if there is no tomorrow.

Avoidance Or Denial?

The conversation went something like this:

Question: I notice that your legs are bent and you try not to put any weight on them when you use your walker. Why is that?

Answer: I'm not sure.

Question: Do you experience pain when you walk?

Answer: Not really, sometimes, not really.

Question: You mentioned that you give yourself a shot every day. What is that for?

Answer: I think it's for - I forget.

Question: You said you went to your primary

care doctor to see about a back operation that you have been told may help you. What did she say?

Answer: She said I couldn't have it.

Question: Why?

Answer: She didn't say.

This lovely woman has three children. All of them are professionals and live near her. One is a doctor. Where are they during their parent's time of need?

Sometimes you have to ask the question to get the answer. Sometimes you ask the question and still don't get the answer.

Heaven Or Hell? Depends On Your Point Of View.

The group of five middle-aged women parked their cars along the tree-lined street and breathed in the hot air of summer. Crunching dead magnolia leaves under their feet as they walked along the sidewalk, they all chattered at once like a gang of teenage girls. If their own daughters were talking in a similar fashion, the group would have just ever so slightly and ever so judgmentally rolled their eyes and tut-tutted to themselves.

But this group was excited to be going to an assisted living community to give its dozen or so occupants hand massages. The group had decided that a visit was "just what the gals who live here would need," suggested the leader. Stepping almost in unison, they approached the wide, white veranda that wrapped itself around its rocking chair occupants. The old mansion-like home was nestled among a residential area and if you weren't looking for it, you would never know it was there.

The rocker occupants neither smiled nor frowned. They seemed to be whispering among themselves about these approaching women.

Once inside, the "younger seniors" set up shop - tables, chairs, bottles of hand lotion, rings off their fingers and a smile on their faces. The first of the "older seniors" came forth and readily thrust her hand into the hand of the younger woman. "I haven't had a hand massage in over twenty years! This feels so good!" It gave pause to the younger woman.

Twenty years, she thought. Wow! And she had one at least every other week, she reminisced. She suddenly felt guilty without understanding why.

The second senior left her ring on saying, "I promised my husband I would never take it off and it's been sixty years. I don't plan to break that promise now."

The younger senior thought to herself. She wasn't even that old, let alone married that long.

They continued to stream in. It took three pushes for one of the rocking chair occupants to get out of the rocker on the porch. Then a few jerky steps to steady themselves for the walk into the activity room where the hand lotion was being dispensed.

One of the last ones to enter was a small, pleasant woman who kept up a steady, rhythmic conversation with the younger senior. As they talked about the weather, her children, what she used to do as a younger woman, etc., it inevitably turned to inquiring how long the senior had lived in the community. "Oh, about six months, I guess," she sighed.

"It seems like a beautiful place to live and some nice people to live with," the younger senior commented as she finished up the hand massage.

"Yes, dear, I guess it is. If you don't mind being confined."

How much do we really understand what another person is going through as they age?

The Recliner Jockey

"Brace yourself! He's a mean one!" The expression on the former caregiver's face was serious with eyebrows crawling toward each other like two plucked caterpillars and her eyes squinting into small slits as if she were caught in the headlights of an on-coming car. "And he owns a gun. I saw it myself," she half shouted in a high pitched voice to anyone who would listen to her at the meeting table. We were all listening. "It's a 9mm," she added. Wondering how she knew one gun from the other, I glanced at the representative of the state who was in attendance, as he reluctantly nodded his head. He looked like one of those dolls you see in the back of some cars

– the head seemingly not attached to the body but floating as if on its own. The caregiver's comments obviously pained him. I wasn't sure if he was pained to hear this information for himself or if he was upset that the rest of us were hearing it.

I had been asked to this meeting to see if I would help. The local health care agency had acquired this gentleman as a client and they needed an overseer of his care. I decided to take the chance and agreed to see the gentleman in question on a regular but temporary basis. They needed an advocate to make sure all of his needs were being met. Was the lawn at his two-bedroom home being maintained by the handyman the agency had hired? Was the twenty-four hour caregiver doing her job? Was food in the house and was he being bathed on a regular basis. Sounded pretty simple. I wondered why there was so much consternation with this fellow.

Upon meeting him, it was obvious why no one liked to visit him. As I walked toward the fifty-year-old red brick home with its gravel driveway, a Certified Nursing Assistant was hurrying down the short ramp that led away from his front door. The door slammed. A window shade was slightly lifted, two squinty eyes peered out and, just as quickly, the shade slammed shut. The C.N.A. shouted over her shoulder, never breaking her stride as she headed straight toward her car, "Good luck, girl. You're going to need it."

This greeting made for an interesting start. When I knocked on the door, I swore that it was still vibrating from the previous visitor's slam. Another C.N.A. answered the door. With an apologetic look on her face, she opened the door wider and I stepped into a dark, closed-up room that at one time had served as a living room in this small home.

It served a new purpose now. Now it contained a hospital bed that was pushed into a corner. There was no bedspread and no pillow, just some worn sheets haphazardly covering an old mattress. An even older recliner, holding its brooding occupant, was shoved near a TV stand that housed the constant companions of the aging, chair-bound senior - the tissue box, the trashcan, the dog-eared television schedule, and the clock.

The chair's occupant looked up and growled, "I don't know you." I responded, "No, you don't.

But this is your lucky day. You get to meet me."
He did not smile. He did not comment.

My eyes quickly scanned the room checking for the gun.

I sat down next to him and explained who I was and what I was there to do for him. He promptly told me that I wasn't needed, and I promptly told him that he had no say in the deal. "Besides," I sniffed, "you'd be crazy to turn down a visit from any woman. What's wrong with you anyway?"

He took that in for a moment and studied me so hard that I felt my fillings beginning to melt. I kept looking for the gun.

Then, what do you know? He smiled. Seemed he liked a smarty-pants and he had met his match.

We talked about how he hated his family. And when he balled up his fist and cursed them, I just listened. When he spit into a can that was near his chair, I patted his arthritic knee.

His world was this room with its dusty shades, ancient curtains, and a recliner that was as cantankerous as he was. It moaned as often as he did. Sometimes it worked and sometimes it didn't. And the material was so worn and faded that the original color was no longer obvious.

He had one love. He was an exceptional bike rider. He won many, many medals in the senior division of the local bike races. "Look under the TV set and bring out that plastic bag," he barked. Inside the bag were over a dozen medals. Medals of accomplishments. He was still winning them up to a few years ago. He was in his early eighties when the stroke hit him. He went from riding the wind to slugging it out daily with an ancient chair. A recliner jockey. He hated it. No wind in his face, no legs pumping, no turning to look back to see whom he had passed in the race.

This was a new race now - a race with life. Or a race with death. The only wind was from the ancient oscillating fan across the room. The emphysema wouldn't let his legs even walk, let alone pump. He couldn't even get out of the chair by himself. From on top of the world to the seat of the chair. It was not fair.

Life can be snatched out from under you without so much as a warning. Are you living life to the fullest...right now?

Nothing A Little Makeup Can't Fix.

The house and its owner reflected each other. Funny how those things start to happen as we age.

The home was neglected and needed a good scrubbing. So did its owner.

The grass was cut but was not trimmed or mulched around what used to be flowerbeds. The owner's hair was recently washed but simply pulled back with a red, plastic hair band that looked as if it had been living at the bottom of the sock drawer somewhere, neglected but back in use at least for the moment.

The driveway had cracks running through the concrete with bits of neglected weeds reaching seeded heads skyward as infrequent visitors stepped on them from time to time.

The owner's face had years and years of lines running pell-mell from cheek to cheek and from one side of her forehead to the other, leading to nowhere in particular but each line with a story.

The painting on the house was old and faded. It could be spruced up quite nicely with some new paint, maybe a pale shade of yellow or blue.

The owner had made an attempt to paint her lips with a lipstick of obvious and dubious ancient origin. Its bright red color did not match her pink top that had the hem coming out of it. But the deliberate attempt to put on some makeup produced an unsteady streak across her lips that filled in the cracks around her mouth. A small amount landed on her front, crooked tooth. She was proud of the attempt. It had been quite a while since she had to "dress up."

On the fence was a hard-to-read sign dangling from a rusty nail. It seemed to have once read, "Beware of the dog." Of course, there was no longer a dog.

The look on the owner's face could have been a sign that read, *stay away*. But the real sign was revealed during our conversation. It could have said, *"Scared to death of being alone."* This sign would be worn on her face for all to see for the rest of her life.

What we think we are not saying is being screamed from another direction.

Mantra Man

I called him "Mantra Man." If he repeated his mantra one more time to his mother, I thought I would scream.

As an only child who lived several states away from his mother, he was her source of comfort, guidance and reassurance. When his father was alive this was not a problem. In fact, the son said it was a pleasure to confirm their decisions. After all, he really wasn't making their decisions for them. He was being told after the fact. That was fine with him. He was busy. And "whatever mama wanted" was always ok.

But Dad died. And he died suddenly. Only then did the son realize how handicapped his mother really was.

His parents had been married for almost sixty years. She was eighty-five years old and she had never written a check. She had never driven a car nor had she ever taken the fifty-pound dog to the vet by herself. And somehow the grass "just got cut" without her so much as even thinking about it when her husband was alive. But that all changed when her husband died so suddenly.

So she called the only source of comfort she knew, the son who lived so far away. Mantra Man. "Whatever you want, Mama."

No matter what she asked or what she said, his answer was always the same. "Whatever you want, Mama." Her questions were different and frightening now. She was facing decisions, many new ones, which she never had to face alone before. But the answer never changed. "Whatever you want, Mama."

She was scared but trying not to show it. He didn't want to see it. All sorts of questions but always the same mantra… "Whatever you want, Mama."

Should I open a checking account?

The lawn company didn't show up to cut the grass. Who do I call?

My friends can't take me to the store today and I'm low on food. What should I do?

Should I sell the house? The real estate agent says I need to. Do I?

"Whatever you want, Mama."

The real estate agent talked to Mama for three long hours. While it was not what Mama wanted to talk about, it was so wonderful to have anyone to talk to. So when the agent said, "Just sign here," Mama signed.

Mama did not have another place to live. She did not know how to call a mover. She did not know how to rent or buy another place. She did not know how to handle the $300,000.00 that she received from the sale of the too big house that she and her husband lived in for so long.

"Did I do the right thing, Son?"

"Whatever you want, Mama."

Are we hearing our seniors or merely listening to them?

The Right To Vote!

He prided himself on raising his children to appreciate this country. He taught them to respect authority, to question what didn't seem right, to help the helpless and to vote. "Above all else, make sure you vote and don't ever take that privilege for granted." I heard him repeat this to his children when they were young. He repeated himself again as they turned eighteen and they all drove together for the first time to vote as a family. "Educate yourself on what the issues are and what the candidate is promising. Then vote!"

Now, as an old, sick man, too weak to get out of bed, his head was laying softly on a white, down-filled pillow. The pillow was covered with a monogrammed pillowcase - one that had been in the family for a very long time and whose lace-trimmed edges were frayed. It had been in the family so long he couldn't remember when his now deceased wife bought it. "It's always been around, like I have," he chuckled softly. He always spoke softly. "I can't ever remember him raising his voice to any of us," his daughter said as she held his limp hand. Tears filled her eyes as she looked at her dying father. He gazed back at her and asked her what day it was. "November 7th, Papa," she said.

"Ah, yes, election day," he said. "Where is my voting ballot?" His daughter smiled as she said she knew he would ask for it. She slipped it into his hand. He was the only left-handed member of the family. He carefully balanced the pen to make a mark on the ballot. Then he signed it. His shaking hands gave it to his only daughter who smiled, knowing whom he had voted for. Putting the ballot in her purse, she promised to deliver it that evening before the cut-off time. She stroked his hand gently, then brought it to her lips and softly kissed his fingers. He was too weak to do anything other than smile and whisper a soft "Thank you, dear."

The next afternoon I received a call from his daughter. "He died last night shortly after the votes were counted. His man won!" We both softly cried and laughed at the same time. She realized that the last thing he signed while still alive was his last voting ballot. A fitting exit, don't you think?

This generation of seniors understands what the right to vote really means.

Giving Up, Giving Out, Moving On.

Her anger filled her heart. She had so much anger it filled the room. For the tenth day in a row she had spent endless hours with her dying mother. Hours of holding her withered blue-veined hands - hands that no longer flowed with life sustaining blood. Hours of applying sweet smelling body lotion on blotched, swollen feet attached to tiny, flesh-colored balloons where toes used to be. Hours trying to coax just one more bite into a mouth that could barely open through cracked, caked lips, let alone chew and swallow. Hours of helping the helpless on and off the bedside commode only to have to clean up urine that didn't quite make it. "But that's ok, Mom, don't worry." Not that Mom worried. She wasn't coherent enough to worry. Her body had given out and given up. It is the only time in her eighty-two years that her family had witnessed this depression-era diva give up on anything.

Her daughter was angry. Angry at her uncaring husband who was more interested in his club meetings than visiting a dying old lady or having a pot of hot soup on the table after she made the hour-long trip home alone…again…in the dark…. crying, crying, crying. She was angry at life, and she was furious at death and what it made the living become.

The "stuff" of our culture becomes the invaders when one is dying. Electric lights become too bright. Food is too difficult and tasteless. Clothes are big, clumsy and not really necessary. Jewelry is a hazard, makeup a joke. Nothing makes sense when you are dying. The way you die, the reason you die and certainly how you die makes no sense at all. How could it?

Most of us are born into this world surrounded by love, hope and with family members who are full of excitement and expectation. Even strangers surround us and cuddle us and want to hold us as they say we smell like a baby and everyone smiles and nods in understanding and agreement. Someone might even say, "boy, if we could bottle that smell we'd make a mint." And everyone in the room would chuckle and say, "Me next! Me next! Let me hold her."

When we die we are surrounded by tubes, bland food, stark walls, piped-in music, fear and hospital gowns that opens in the back, exposing us to the world. People rub our hands and cry. No one likes the smell and no one wants to hold us. And everyone fears us because they know they are next.

Dying must be very, very lonely but the dying don't tell us. No matter how many people join the parade of visitors and family members, not any of us can appreciate how difficult it must be to check out. It doesn't even matter if we believe we are going to a better place, another dimension or we just stop breathing, it is still something we do alone, with no one having the hope, excitement or expectation that we experienced when we first arrived. This time it's different. And it's scary no matter what our faith. We do it alone with the chemicals, the tubes, the glaring lights and without our son-in-law caring. The daughter remains angry.

What do we really know about death?

Little Old Ladies Discussing The Market

To the casual observer, they looked like what American society would call "two little old ladies." Both had gray hair. Both had to be in their eighties. Their chairs faced each other so close together that their knees almost touched. The stronger of the two took the hands of the weaker one. They put their heads closer together so they could hear each other because neither one could hear very well. In actuality, the intimate-looking gestures were those gestures of necessity.

The stronger one (the visitor) was gently rubbing her thumbs over the tops of the hands of the weaker one (the patient). Thumbs ran over the tiny hills and valleys created by the large, black and blue veins. A flesh colored bandage circled the right thumb where one more battle scar was forming due to a recent fall. Falls are so common with "little old ladies."

The weaker one was still in her sleepwear – a soft, white robe with pink trim and fuzzy socks that matched. She had not been dressed for weeks. "Too much effort." She sighed, gently and slowly shaking her head from side to side. The other one nodded in agreement so that they looked as if they were contradicting each other. One head going up and down, and the other head going back and forth.

The stronger one understood the words "too much." Her own arthritis made buttoning her favorite purple blouse difficult so she could empathize somewhat.

To the casual observer they seemed lost in their *old* world. But upon close examination, if you were privy to their conversation, you would hear them discussing the newspaper headlines, the latest war issues and what their stocks were doing that particular day. Interspersed were conversations of grandchildren and great grandchildren. There was such a contrast in what the observer was seeing versus what they were hearing!

Soon the weak one stopped talking. She withdrew her hand from the four-handed clasp. She leaned back in her lounge chair – her home away from home that it had become out of necessity.

She closed her eyes and soon her breathing took up a soft cadence of its own. In her drug-induced slumber, she silently dismissed her visitors while she enjoyed the journey where only strong pain medication could take her. Gone were the stock market quotes, the latest headline discussions and any hope of further conversation, at least for that day.

Strong and weak parted ways until the drugs wore off and the weak one would re-surface.

Truly, you can't judge a book by its cover.

Canes And Pierced Ears

The crowd of five hundred seniors gathered to hear the speaker. But first the young high school color guard silently marched in and presented the American flag. All five hundred seniors stood with their hands over their hearts.

Drum-ba-da-drum.

Walking in tight formation and to the beat of the drummer, the contrast between the young and the old could not be more pronounced.

Drum-ba-da-drum.

Young straight backs held heavy state and national flags while older, stooped backs leaned their veined hands on the chairs in front of them for support.

The flutes, the drums and the sharp-stepping flag carriers kept the beat as the drummer beat out the cadence.

Drum-ba-da-drum.

The rhythmic click of the cadence matched the click of the color guards' heels on the wooden floor.

Drum-ba-da-drum, click-clickity-click.

More contrasts. One group was young, with barely a hint of peach fuzz sprouting on their faces that would soon give way to manhood. A small earring in the shape of a spike peaked out from the tall, plumed majorette hat. The earring seemed to take on a life of its own - as if it were trying to wiggle free from its confinement in order to see the ceremony for itself.

The other group was mostly gray headed and not as tall as they used to be. But if you looked closely, you could actually see a few growing momentarily taller with the aid of a cane as the flag passed by.

As the flutes and drums paid homage to the prominent American flag, wrinkled hands slowly rose to rest upon every heart. From somewhere in the cavernous room a low murmur slowly and almost imperceptibly at first, began to come alive. Soft and gentle, it began to slowly skip through the room as it gathered voices and volume until the instruments and the voices were one. The Star Spangled Banner wrapped its arms around everyone in the room that day.

Many had their eyes closed. Some swayed on their canes and a few silent tears ran through crinkled lines that provided small trenches on withered cheeks. You could almost see their wars: World War II, Korea, Viet Nam, September 11, Afghanistan, Iraq.

As the song gained crescendo, as the tears left stains on shirtfronts, everyone in the room remembered and sang. At the last note, a short silent pause seemed to be revering the moment. But just as quickly, old hands became strong again as canes were dropped, smiles abounded and applause spontaneously broke out among both young and old.

The speaker approached the podium even while the applause still hung in the air. "God bless America!" he shouted. It seemed to be the only appropriate words.

Memories of wars lost and won never fade away.

FREE BONUS

52 tips to help you communicate with your parents. — Worth $49.95

One of the biggest issues adult children face is how to approach their parents on issues of aging. They question themselves with concerns such as, "how do I approach my dad about his erratic driving? I'm afraid to let my children ride with him anymore." Or maybe they are thinking, "I know my parents need help but I don't know how to bring up the subject without sounding like I want to take over their lives...I really don't! But how do I start?"

This booklet is chock full of tips on how to approach your parents about a variety of senior concerns. Delicate topics such as: where do they want to live their senior years, what is the difference between alternative living communities, is there a way for my elderly mother to remain in her home with some help that doesn't cost too much, and is there a way a senior can volunteer without having to spend money or drive anywhere?

These fifty-two tips provide suggestions and options that will assist the adult child as they help their parents approach the numerous aspects of aging.

Yours to download free with the purchase of this book. Go to www.speakingonaging.com and get your copy today and thank you for buying Unwrapping the Sandwich Generation.

Happy aging!

Organizing your world... your way

PEACE OF MIND
for you and your loved ones!

Preparing for the future for you and your loved ones can be:

- Confusing
- Stressful on everyone
- Difficult trying to track scattered information
- Complicated trying to find & compile important information
- Too complex to easily communicate to family members

The question...

How can I face the future, find the information my family needs, put it all together and do it stress-free?

The answer...

Life*information*™: Organizing your world...your way is a handsome binder providing a method and a place for all your important personal information.

Life*information*™ is:

- A beautifully bound classic black binder
- Ten personal information chapters
- Organized & Comprehensive
- The Place for your essential information such as medical, financial, legal, spiritual, personal wishes and desires and much more
- Easy to complete with adult family members or alone
- Peace of mind for you and your family. No more stress or guessing what you want or where to find it; it's all written out and clear.

Life*information*™ Binders are available in two timeless styles for your convenience.

THE CLASSIC (for one person)
- Ten information chapters
- Sectional tabs
- Bound in black
- Three ring binder format
- Front inside pockets
- An investment of $99.95 plus tax, shipping and handling

THE DELUXE (for two people)
- Ten information chapters
- Sectional tabs
- Front & back inside pockets
- Bound in soft black zippered portfolio
- Legal writing pad
- An investment of $129.95 plus tax, shipping and handling

Do it for yourself, but more importantly, do it for your family.
Don't wait for a crisis to occur and wish you had taken care of your loved ones!

Order yours today! Call 757.496.4722

Printed in the USA
CPSIA information can be obtained
at www.ICGtesting.com
JSHW012015140824
68134JS00025B/2426